THE MEMOIRS OF PASTOR MARTINUS METGOD:

MY REMARKABLE YEAR WITH CASE PARKER

KEES POSTMA

Also by Kees Postma

The Retreat: A light-hearted and humorous story about a soul searching Pastor (Pastor Case Parker Series: Part I)

The Heaven on Earth Conference: The Wondrous diary of an
Ordinary Pastor

(Pastor Case Parker Series: Part II)

PROLOGUE

"Peter, come quickly, see what I found here." My sister Elizabeth turned her and my life upside down with those eight words. Of course, she did not know it at the time, as is often the case with life-changing words and events. They are only understood and appreciated in retrospect.

She had uttered those words from the dusty and musty-smelling attic of the parsonage. The place where my father breathed his last. Not in the attic, of course, but just below it on the second floor, in an austere bedroom stripped of all luxury. A short illness had ended his long agony ten days ago. That agony had not begun with his physical deterioration but with the procedure concerning his pastoral termination, which had begun more than two decades ago.

My father, according to the board of his denomination, had fallen into what they called "gross and impermissible sin" and did not provide enough evidence to prove otherwise. They had to let him go, they said. A crazy term for describing something that puts a heavy burden on someone and tightens the belt around them and their loved ones unbearably.

"I'll be right with you, sister; it's not a mouse, is it!?" Those critters always used to make her blood run cold. After the Goodwill store had loaded all the furniture, I decided to brave the steep wooden stairs to the attic. The handrail was missing, which made it quite an undertaking for me, even though I'm still in my thirties.

I saw my sister standing over a small wooden box. There was just one among perhaps a hundred cardboard moving boxes full of books. Most of them were covered in dust and only used as references for some sermon series.

The bright sun shone through the poorly insulated roof. A house with authentic elements is what they call it on property websites nowadays. The floorboards creaked as I passed a lot of knickknacks down to Elizabeth, who had placed the box on a small mahogany table. Four thick books with gray covers seemed to be all that was found inside.

I recognized the box immediately. In better times, I made it with my father in the barn. He was serving somewhere in the province of Friesland at the time. With a wood burner, he had engraved a Bible text in it: "Me and my house, we will serve the Lord." I remember well how proudly we walked in and showed it to my mother, Lydia. Elizabeth had not even been born yet.

Although the text was slightly faded, symbolic of how we as a family have fared after Friesland, I still recognized it. The contents, though, were new to me. I grabbed the first book and started flipping through it. I recognized his handwriting from the birthday cards he sent even after Mom, Elizabeth and I had already distanced ourselves from him. He'd always wished us a blessed and joyous year of life, despite it all. He would include his address and phone number in case we still wanted to visit him.

"The Memoirs of Pastor Metgod: My Remarkable Year with Case Parker" was written on the cover in ornate letters. "Crazy title, don't you think Peter?" Elizabeth tended to immediately comment on everything she saw, while I prefer to read for half an hour before jumping to conclusions. "Look, I think this book here deals with the era around the pastoral termination." She spoke in an almost whispered tone, as if a whole battalion of journalists were listening in downstairs. My heart beat erratically like a scratched CD.

I had often wondered how Father got on before and after the verdict of the brethren of the board, who were apparently all born before the fall and thus perfect. Something in me wanted nothing more than to leave that place, the memoir. What was done was done. Away from the memory of a marriage shattered by one fatal mistake. From a parental home in ruins. Still, curiosity won out over my hunched shoulders and shallow breathing. This memoir would surely provide answers to questions I never asked, but it would probably also shine a new light on Father. Did we see him in his true colors or was there more than met the eye?

I hoped for answers to questions I had asked over the past few years. Whether he died as lonely as I have imagined. Whether he committed that gross and intolerable sin, or if it was simply one big misunderstanding. A perfect storm in a murky glass of water. Whether he missed me as much as I missed him.

From the pulpit, father had been a celebrated orator; at home, he seemed trapped in a world without words. Especially during the agony of his pastoral termination. It was difficult for him to express his soulful feelings. As a result, he was often unreachable to Mother. He seemed unable to speak the language of the heart and emotions.

"You take this part home, Peter, and I'll take care of the first three, and we can swap later." Elizabeth said as we carefully walk down the stairs together. I hesitated but decided to bite the bullet. We walked through the large hall with the marble floor to the old wooden door with stained glass and a gilded lock.

The books in moving boxes would be picked up later today by the church administrator. In a letter, he announced that today things needed to be in order because a new pastor couple was moving into the rectory the next week. Case Parker, Dad's last intern twenty years back, and his wife, Deborah, would take over. As the son of a former Baptist pastor, I wished them well. I closed the door for the last time with the memoirs in my hands, not knowing that with it, a whole new world would open for me.

CHAPTER 1

THE INTRODUCTION

Dear Reader. Welcome to the final part of my memoir. It is the year 2024, and I have undoubtedly entered the winter of my life. The other three seasons passed far too quickly. No snowy fun, more like endless rain from a gray cloud cover, if you ask me. This home stretch is the hardest for me.

I have now lost more than I own and forgotten more than I have remembered. As a pensioned pastor, the great looking back has begun. Indeed, in human terms, more lies behind me than before me. It is time to delight the world with this final part of my memoirs. But maybe I am aiming too high. I hope Peter recognizes the box to which I will entrust this final work. Hope he and Elizabeth are well.

This last part is about a special period in my ministry, beginning in 2004. My colleagues, behind my back, called it "the long agony of Martinus Metgod." I had already been declared guilty by them because I chose not to vigorously defend myself against the accusations made against me. Where there is smoke, there is fire, they must have thought. They failed to remember that we serve a Lord who did not open His mouth either. I do not want to compare my case with His, though. He was tempted but did not sin. That cannot be said of me, though I am innocent of what I have been charged with. At least in part.

Before the problems started, I was known as the golden boy among preachers. As one of the most experienced pastors among Baptists, I was therefore asked by the seminary—in the summer of my life and ministry, the heyday—to accommodate, as a nestor, more than a few interns. Those rascals had to learn the ropes somewhere, and I was more than willing to teach them the nuts and bolts of ministry. Some made a lasting impression, and I expected them to hit the ground running. Others were cut from lesser cloth, and I held out little hope. Sometimes I was wrong, often I was right.

Every now and then someone would come my way who I knew had exceptional talent. Still a little rough around the edges, but with some sharpening, they would be a particularly useful tool in the hands of the Great Carpenter. They made an indelible impression. On me, on the church members, on everyone around them. They were the bubbles in God's champagne, the icing on His cake, the cream of His crop, the sharpest knife in the cutlery drawer. You could tell by everything that they were destined for the pulpit or predestined for pastoral care. They passed every aspect with flying colors. You only meet people like this occasionally.

The last intern I had the privilege of mentoring, Case Parker, was not one of those people. He was the skirting board missing from every living room, the door creaking, the shelf sagging. At least at first glance. If I remember correctly, he was born in the province of Drenthe, descended from a lineage of ditchers and peat cutters. He was not fluent in Dutch, and personal hygiene was not a high priority for this gentleman. I have sometimes thought that knife and fork were simply not found in the Parker home growing up. You cannot really blame a boy like that. It often takes five generations for families like that to get back in line with the rest of the Netherlands.

Yet even such a person deserves a chance. Blunt skates can be sharpened. If God can speak through donkeys, then surely the Almighty must also be able to speak through people from Drenthe, I thought, when I laid eyes on his handwritten scribbles.

My wife, Lydia, God rest her soul, convinced me that I could take this boy under my wings for a season. You could not expect anything else from her. As a child, she used to bring in everything that was hurt and wingless. Even as a pastor's wife, she always had a big heart for the sick, weak, and damaged part of the flock. She knew mercy, upon mercy, upon mercy. The kindness of Christ was found in her much more than in me.

I let her convince me, and partly because of this, it became a wonderful year in which, on the one hand, young Case scared me with his stupidity. On the other hand, I could not help but take him into my heart. Other interns were fire, lightning, and thunder. He turned out, in retrospect, to be the gentle voice in which the voice of that Other one was audible.

The timing of his arrival seemed a bit unfortunate at first. My elders had just informed the congregation that they had forwarded a report of inappropriate behavior against me to the National Baptist Board; I will talk more about that later. Lydia and I both had no idea what they were on about. She a little less than I, I must admit. I thought it would probably blow over. It did not.

The great speculation began. People, understandably, wondered what could be going on with their pastor. Was my leadership style too authoritarian? Had I been guilty of verbal harassment? Had I grabbed a brother by the throat, falsified minutes, withheld offering funds? Had I indulged in child abuse or an extramarital affair? I felt their piercing eyes like lashes on my back, their whispers were like Judas's kiss.

So, I wrote the Drent a handwritten letter that an internship with a suspected, under-the-magnifying-glass pastor might be a little too much spectacle for his tender soul. "This may get nasty, Case; you may decide to give up your career as a pastor before it has even begun."

Two days later, he called. It was a very pleasant conversation in which he informed me that he would never again have the chance to experience such a process up close, so that he would still like to come to Zwagerheide. Lydia listened in and nodded, and I could do nothing but give my consent.

Less than four days later, sometime in September, he showed up at our doorstep. It was on a Monday morning. I was sitting in the study, clearing my inbox, when I heard a low hum outside that increased as time passed. It ended abruptly just in front of the parsonage. I heard a car door open, then slam shut again.

Curious, I looked through the window and saw a young man, about twenty-five years old at the most, walking into the yard. The bell rang, and I heard Lydia put down her things in the kitchen to unlock the door. Her voice was cheerful, welcoming as ever. A moment later, I heard two pairs of footsteps approaching, and there was a knock on my office door. The youngster stood jovially in the doorway with his arms open, waiting for a hug, it seemed.

He must have been almost two meters. At least that is what it looked like in the old narrow door. He was wearing a pair of black Nike Air Max with white Umbro socks that stuck halfway up his lower legs. His knees were battered. Afterwards he confided to me that this was from a brick laying job he had completed at a friends' house on Saturday. Frayed jean shorts and a sleeveless black shirt that read "teach me to carry my burdens" completed the look. His smile was wide and generous, his eyes were bright, beautifully blue too, and I could not help but stand up and take him, also literally, in my arms. Being a bit shorter, I briefly got lost somewhere in his armpit hair, to Lydia's hilarity.

"Well, pastor, here I am. Case Parker, weighing in at two hundred pounds. Even though you got yourself into quite a bit of trouble, Martinus, I think I could learn quite a bit from you. Maybe you can learn a thing or two from me too. Who knows, right?"

I immediately wondered if Case might not understand boundaries by quickly becoming so personal, just like that. Respect for an old geezer in the ministry was nowhere to be seen. But it was also disarming. No one had put a rigid straitjacket on him yet. They had not even managed that at the seminary. He had become special by remaining himself. "True, Case. Summer is over, and autumn seems to have arrived. I am dealing with some headwinds, but that will all blow over, boy. Come, I will take you to Sister Wierenga. Yesterday, after the service, she told me that your room is ready."

With an "Okey dokey, let's go" on his part, we walked together to the roaring monster parked on the sidewalk while Lydia watched us from the house.

"Isn't she beautiful, pastor?" Case asked, pointing at the loud vehicle that had announced his arrival. "I bet you've never driven a VW Golf VR6 2.9 liter, finished in dragon green metallic with BBS alloy wire wheels and over 190 horsepower under the hood."

He had won that bet. He tossed me the keys, and before I knew it, I was seated in a kind of ejector seat with dual belts and gripping the leather steering wheel tightly. With a small hand movement, I brought the monster to life. The dual exhaust produced so much vibration that it felt like the earth had begun to tremble. Its sound was almost drowned out by the blissful echoes of "The Power of Your Love" booming from the speakers. "Nice sound, right Martinus? It is a high-end subwoofer set I had installed in the back. A double high-end tweeter and woofer, including an acoustic damping package. It costs me a fortune, but it is worth it, pastor."

I wondered if God ever foresaw that He would be worshiped in this way in Drenthe and surrounding areas. Probably so; nothing escapes His notice.

Fortunately, it was only a short drive to Sister Wierenga's place, but even then, anything could go wrong. Because of young Case's ambush so early after my day of preaching, I had completely forgotten that there was a funeral at the Reformed Church that morning. After I had taken about three-speed bumps, at Case's request, diagonally so as not to damage the lowered car, disaster struck.

As I wanted to turn left, I saw the hearse approaching with about a hundred Reformed people dressed in black in its wake. There was no way for me to turn. The usher was leading with a serious face, and his seconds had blocked the option of going straight and turning right. I could already see some in the funeral procession looking our way, angry and indignant. Now Reformed people look gloomy most of the time, even when singing "Praise the Lord, with a Joyful Sound," but here they certainly had a point.

This was only made worse when Case, without deliberation, jumped out of the passenger seat and got into position next to the VW Golf with his hand on his chest. As best he could, he tried to sing the first verse of our National Anthem, "The Wilhelmus." He did more than enough to make the angels weep, I suppose.

I tried to nip it in the bud and snapped at him that in the province of Drenthe it may be normal to hurl an anthem at mourners, but we do not do that over here. As I bent over the shifter to pull him in by his jean shorts with all my might, I accidentally kicked the gas pedal. I inadvertently whipped the VR6 engine to 8,000 RPM, to the horror of the weeping widow and her grown children.

What I did not know is that you could create the so-called "pop and bang" sound by doing so. The exhaust popped three times exactly as the hearse passed. I tried to hide behind the two large plush dice hanging from the rearview mirror, but without the desired effect. If looks could kill, there would be another funeral in five days, and this time not from the Reformed congregation.

Huddled up, I suddenly heard Case urging the procession to calm down. "Steady as you go, do not let us keep you, dear mourners. Reverend Metgod in there is still a virgin when it comes to horsepower, that is. He insisted on going for a ride and does not always oversee the consequences of his actions. On behalf of him and the Baptist church, my sincere apologies, and we wish you all a very pleasant funeral," he spoke in the tone of a flight attendant who had just blared safety instructions through the plane for the thousandth time while knowing no one is listening. This incident would become exemplary of our collaboration. Sister Wierenga could write her own memoirs about it, I'm sure.

Like me, she enjoyed Case's presence. Despite things shattering into a thousand pieces at home and in the church, Case brought laughter. Case grabbed every opportunity to serve with both hands. Unlike me, where more opportunities slipped between my fingers each time. At first glance, I did not see much in him; I would be surprised.

This week, twenty years after our first meeting, I received another handwritten letter from Case in which he casually mentioned that he is struggling with symptoms of depression and burnout and is about to leave for Ireland for a three-day retreat. It was the cue for me to begin this memoir. You never know when winter, too, will take its last cold breath and the grayness will turn to clear, blue skies.

I will use the pristine white of this paper to outline to you my remarkable year with Case Parker. I hope you can take a punch. I estimate that you can learn much more from our mistakes than what went right in our lives that year. Perhaps this last part will also give the children peace of mind to know what had gotten into their father. The truth will surely set them free.

Be blessed,

Br. Metgod, Zwagerheide

Chapter 2

The Indictment

The long agony of my pastoral termination began much earlier than my suspicious colleagues thought. The letter I received from the national board was just another step in a process that, until then, had taken place only in the twilight of my inner life, far from church members, as well as Lydia and the children. My waters were still, but the grounds infinitely deep. What followed was only the logical consequence of my own straying. What is kindled will one day burst open.

I have always thought that godly men and women made terrible mistakes in a fit of insanity. Those "I don't know what got into me" moments. Now I know that these things happen gradually. It is like a staircase of fourteen steps toward a raging ocean where the waves crash against the cliffs every thirty seconds. You know in your right mind, there at the top of those steps, that you must be crazy to dive in.

At the same time, it has a great appeal. How cold would the water be? Could you swim against the current with everything inside of you? What would it be like to be carried away on those waves? Within a few minutes of daydreaming, you decide to carefully take the first two steps down. You feel the temperature drop as the sun no longer touches you and the drops of water caress your face. The sound of the waves hitting the rocks is louder than up there. You are hidden from view, no passerby seeing you. It is quite nice here, not as bad as you had thought. You have taken the first steps down and you are still doing well.

But what would happen if you descended two, three, or four more steps? The stone steps just below you are still dry. There is no danger of slipping. The water will not come up that high, and if it does, you can always go back up, right? Just be cautious. You are in control. You feel your heart rate increase slightly as you descend and get closer and closer to the ocean. The foam flies around your ears, the sea roars, you are alive. All your senses are stimulated to the max. You can already taste the salt water on your tongue.

The "Do Not Proceed" sign can be overlooked. There is more than common sense. Even the plaque with names whose lives the sea has taken does not cause any alarms: You are stronger than they were. Something that feels so right cannot be wrong, can it? You slowly take off your clothes as you take the last steps and fall forward.

The water is colder than imagined. You lose control, your breath stops. In twenty seconds, the rhythm of the sea will introduce you to the rugged ancient cliffs. What you did not know up there now begins to dawn on you. You are no match for the sea. No matter how attractive she looked from above, now she has wrapped her tentacles around you, and you are at her mercy. The blow against the cliff you do not overcome, a woeful death. The sea has seduced and won and is already looking up at the next curious spectator who marvels at her power as your name is added to the memorial plaque.

In the words of Psalm 1, dear readers: I walked, I stood by, and I sat down. I took this first step toward the abyss during what is nowadays called the midlife crisis. In retrospect, I would have been better off buying a motorcycle, running a marathon, or climbing Kilimanjaro.

In the first half of my life, I came, saw, and conquered. A good education, lovely wife and two children. One of each kind. A "millionaires' family" is what they call it in the English-speaking world. Academically, I was a golden boy, and the world was at my feet. I quickly climbed the Baptist equivalent of the career ladder and was known as the Crown Prince of Baptist preachers.

I was enjoying the game, stringing together highlights, until the referee whistled, and the first half of my life was complete history. I found myself in the twilight zone between the first and second half. But I would not call it a rest or a break. No warm stove, a cup of tea, or an encouraging pat from the coach. I panicked, became unsure, distanced myself, did not know where to look.

Lydia put her finger on the sore spot at the time. "You may have climbed the ladder, Martinus, but you didn't see that it was against the wrong wall." She was right. If I had as much ambition toward those under my own roof as outside it, it might have all worked out. But the bride of Christ was more important to me than my own. I call this spiritual cheating. Many of my colleagues at that time were guilty of it. I am sure it is still like that. Not much has changed since, I suppose.

What happened to me spiritually in those days turned out to be a harbinger of what was still to come. Sin. The gross inadmissible sin, as my superiors called it. In a letter I received from them, they described it this way:

* * *

Aug. 23, 2004

Dear Brother Metgod,

We regret to inform you that a formal complaint has been filed against you by your council of elders. It is suspected that you have behaved inappropriately toward a female member of the congregation. Your council of elders, after its own investigation, has sought our advice, and we have jointly arrived at this first formal step.

You know that, upon the presumption of an urgent reason for termination of employment, you can be suspended as a pastor. Indecent behavior is such a reason, according to Article 3.1. However, the congregation and our board first want to give you the opportunity to defend yourself against this accusation. You have the freedom to be assisted by an attorney.

Should the presumption prove unfounded, you will be rehabilitated by the church, which will be communicated or confirmed to you in writing.

Pending the investigation, you will initially be placed on suspension with pay for fourteen days. We trust that we have given you sufficient information. We wish you His nearness and wisdom in the weeks to come.

Brotherly greetings,

The investigation committee

* * *

"So, pastor, spit it out. I don't like to be kept in the dark for so long. You indicated in your letter that the timing of my arrival is a bit unfortunate because of 'certain imputations.' What kind of mayhem is going on?"

I decided to let Case read the formal indictment, to give him an insight into the raw reality of the world he was about to enter. A forewarned prospective pastor counts for two. It was time to hang out the dirty laundry.

Leaning back with his ankles crossed and his fingers stroking through his scruffy beard, he read the letter intently, sighing, with his eyebrows raised and occasionally looking at me. He spent a few minutes on the writing before folding it up and putting it back into my hands, after which he briefly tested my upper arm with his left fist.

"That's bad news, Martinus. Adulterers and sexual predators do not do very well in the church, I was told in seminary. On the other hand, there is no man overboard, yet, I read. You can still prove them wrong. It will end with a whimper, don't you think?"

"I am afraid not, Case. Even if I am acquitted, people will always think that where there is smoke, there is fire, or at least there must have been. Trust comes on foot and goes on horseback, even among Baptists."

"But if you regret what you did, or better yet repent, Martinus, wouldn't that reassure those gentlemen on the board that you are not as bad as they think you are? Surely the Bible is full of people, like you, who got short-circuited every now and then? David also took a lopsided turn with Bathsheba and notoriously murdered her husband, and he was restored by God and called a man after His own heart. Compared to him, you look just like a baby angel, Martinus.

"Saul chased Christians out of their homes and was complicit in the death of the first martyr, Stephen, before God gave him a new name, heart, and spirit. Peter denied Jesus three times before the rooster crowed but was restored to his position by Jesus Himself. The prodigal son first pretended his father was dead to him by claiming and squandering the inheritance, yet was welcomed with a great feast. Abraham lied for his sake that Sarah was his sister. Rahab was a harlot.

"I could go on and on, Pastor. If there was grace for them all, surely the same will be true for an aging hero of the Baptist Guild of the Netherlands, right? You bet those guys on the board also looked where they had better not look, and I do not think their aim is always true either. Something with tiny specks and big planks, if I recall Jesus." He stared at me with open eyes, like a wagging puppy who had just laid down on his back on command waiting for a cookie. As if with this defense, everything was resolved, and only normal daily business remained.

Was it naivete on the part of young Case, or was the grace he had experienced at his conversion still so fresh and new that he was more familiar with the tenets of our faith? The fact is that, in any case, he did not yet know how church really works. Showing mercy and receiving mercy are two different things.

"We'll talk about it another time Case. Maybe you are right, we'll see. Now that I am on suspension, it means that I must let Thera and Tobias's wedding ceremony pass me by. I will throw you before the lions right away. I asked if they would give you a chance to preach on the most beautiful day of their lives, and they agreed. They will provide a written report on how you did, which you can then add to your portfolio, so the seminary will be happy."

"It will be my first time, Martinus, but as Pippi Longstocking used to say, 'I've never tried that before, so I think I can do it'. You would almost suspect God of a plan that I should be called to Zwagerheide precisely, for a time like this, to do your dirty work, Pastor! Let me just go home and start preparing." After a bang on my other upper arm, as a sign of his love, he shook the dust off his Nikes and left in his humming monster.

In retrospect, I have to say that God did the right thing in placing Case in our midst that year, although that was not reflected in the feedback I received from Thera and Tobias van Ballengooijen after their wedding. Below is their contribution to Case's portfolio.

Dear Brother Metgod,

We were sorry that, because of the ongoing investigation, you were unable to officiate our wedding yourself. It was a wonderful gesture to have your intern do the honors. That boy also needs to get some work done and dive in, and we understand that.

I know that the Holy Scriptures call us to marry only once, but we would like to ask you if you might make an exception. We would like to do it again, under your guidance, when you have proven your innocence. The blessing did not go as planned, to say the least.

Perhaps he was a little nervous because, at the last minute, he also had to lead worship. Our singing Sister Saskia had cancelled a few days before the wedding. In the preliminary discussion, Case had indicated that he was not too bad of a singer and guitar player. We had therefore given him the task of selecting a few suitable songs and leading the worship service. We particularly regret the first part of this assignment. Perhaps you could talk to him about the set list he performed? Below are the chosen songs.

1. *"You Give Love a Bad Name" by Bon Jovi*
2. *"She Drives Me Crazy" by The Fine Young Cannibals*
3. *"I Still Haven't Found What I'm Looking For" by U2*
4. *"Used to Love Her, But I Had to Kill Her" by Guns 'n Roses.*

We should add that some of our unbelieving friends were extremely entertained by this music and Case's playful rendition of it.

Once we had recovered from the music, it was time for the sermon. We had shared with him that after a long time of prayer, we had arrived at the same wedding text as my parents and my grandparents did. Extraordinary, right? Namely, 1 John 4:18-19:

"There is no fear in love. But perfect love drives out fear because fear has to do with punishment. The one who fears is not made perfect in love. We love because he first loved us."

Unfortunately, Brother Parker did not get hold of the right end of the stick. He did choose a text from John, including the fourth chapter and the eighteenth verse. But he did so from the Gospel and not from the first epistle. Here is the text from John 4:18 he preached on:

"The fact is, you have had five husbands, and the man you now have is not your husband. What you have just said is quite true."

Tobias almost fainted when Case explained this verse in detail. All our wedding night, I had to defend myself to Tobias and his family. You know, he comes from a more charismatic background. His father believed that Brother Parker may have spoken a prophetic word, and that my bosom sins of yesteryear have finally come into the light. We had imagined this night quite differently. You will understand.

It is another miracle that it came to a wedding night. Case, after preaching, made a mess of the marriage promises. Just moments before, he had been joltingly trying to link our marriage to the covenant between God and Israel. "As God chose a small, stubborn and headstrong bride, so today you choose Tobias, Thera as your wife."

We only said yes because we knew what he was trying to say.

Still, we would love to get a second chance. Awaiting your reply, pastor.

Thera and Tobias van Ballengooijen.

* * *

Following this report, I did have to speak sternly and admonish Case. I could not do otherwise. But before I did, Lydia and I had to laugh heartily at this report. I decided to reprimand Case the way a father disciplines his child but at the same time enjoys the mischief he does.

I remember one such incident when our Peter was only a toddler. Lydia and I had retreated to the bedroom for a nap when at some point we wondered why we did not hear Peter anymore. As parents, if you leave your child alone to watch the television and do not get called for ten minutes, all alarm bells should go off. Ours went off a little too late.

As we entered the landing and walked down the stairs, we heard him mutter the legendary words "Mmm, yummy chocolate spread!" Once downstairs, we discovered the consequences of our negligence. Like Winnie the Pooh, he sat with his hand in a large jar of chocolate spread, munching deliciously. In between licking, he had managed to coat all the creamy white walls with chocolate, including the kitchen cabinets and the washing machine. As I pointed him out, Lydia and I could not do so without laughing heartily. Similarly, I addressed Case at Sr. Wierenga's kitchen table.

"Yes, Pastor. Point taken. They taught me at seminary that I should take every opportunity to be of service. Since I play guitar, I thought I could do that on the side. Maybe I have taken on a little too much. Church here is sometimes a bit stiff; I thought I would brighten things up a bit. I will pay the newlyweds a visit this afternoon to calm things down, leave that to me.

"Do you know what happened to Sister Saskia? She would not say anything to Thera and Tobias about it, nor to me. A little mysterious, don't you think?"

I hesitated for a moment and gazed out of the window, but decided to tell him the truth. "Saskia filed the complaint against me, Case. I am the subject of the letter, she the object, if you know what I mean. I think this whole thing has ruffled her feathers; all this must have upset her too."

"Okay, that does not surprise me, Pastor. Looked her up in the church directory. Fine-looking woman, a bit younger than you are too, old chum." Case's hand struck my upper arm playfully. "By the way, are you guilty? I do not think I even asked that yet. I gave you a little time to come out with it yourself, but now my curiosity is winning out over my patience, Pastor." He looked at me and did not seem intent on resting his gaze until I had answered.

"That depends on your definition of guilty, Case. Let me put it this way: I feel guilty but disagree that I am guilty of transgressive behavior. It is complicated, kid. I doubt you'll understand. Let us let it rest for now, I am going to call Thera and Tobias and tell them you're coming to bring a big bunch of flowers and a box of expensive chocolate that you paid for out of your own money, I'm sure that will ease things a bit."

CHAPTER 3

FOXES IN THE VINEYARD

Something that has always intrigued me during my conversations with church members is listening to their conversion stories. I remember well when I once shared my own road to Christ as a new believer with an elder from a more liberal church in my village. The only thing he could stammer out was that it was miraculous that you could go from one (unbeliever) to another (believer) in a context like that. He was only concerned with the earthly shift and not the heavenly one. Case shared his story with Lydia and me one evening, and we could conclude nothing else but that it takes all sorts to make a church, and this young man was undeniably His property.

"Actually, it all started when I met Deborah, Pastor. I did not realize it myself at the time, but life is often understood in retrospect, isn't it? She was born and raised in a Christian family, and every now and then, I went along to church. Especially to spend time with her. The rest sounded a bit like higher mathematics. Four years back, I had just turned eighteen, and at the invitation of a friend of Deborah's, we went to a Baptist church a few miles down the road.

"Once there, two things struck me; the abundance of peers

who all had apparently had a life-changing encounter with Jesus and the bad coffee that was served. After the service, I joked that a church with this quality coffee does not expect guests to visit again."

Lydia, with a smile on her face, poured another strong cup of coffee, of the better kind, for Case as he leaned back in my favorite chair and seemed to be picking up steam.

"Yet I became incredibly curious about this Jesus, Pastor. I read on the internet that the church also organized evening services. Brilliant, of course, for heavy drinking Drents like me, you can just sleep in on Sunday morning! I decided to go to church again on a cold December evening. There, the pastor preached on being connected or disconnected to God. As he preached about sin and the holiness of God, it became clear to me that I was disconnected from God. Not that I was a rapist or a murderer as such, but I understood my life revolved around the impure trinity of 'me, myself, and I.' A desire arose within me to connect with God.

'The pastor asked us to bow our heads and close our eyes. When we wanted connection with God, all we had to do was raise our hand and he would pray for us. Upon closing my eyes, something unusual happened. I cannot put it any other way."

Case shifted slightly, and Lydia decided to draw him out a bit. "What do you mean Case, unusual? That is a word from your head, not from your heart. Martinus here is not so good with feelings and emotions either."

I decided not to respond.

"You may not believe this, ma'am, but I saw something while I had my eyes closed. I saw three crosses on a hill. The middle cross was raised and shone brighter than the sun. I was startled and immediately opened my eyes because I thought I had entered some kind of Baptist brainwash get-together. But the longing remained, and when I closed my eyes again, I saw the exact same thing and now also someone standing in front of the cross with his arms wide open. He spoke to me and said, 'Case, you have lived your whole life for yourself, now I want you to walk with me.'

"Madam, I could do nothing but accept His invitation, and do you know what the beautiful thing was? When I opened my eyes, Deborah was sitting next to me crying because she was experiencing a similar thing at that moment. It is unbelievable, isn't it!"

"Did you manage to hold on to that feeling, Case? That feeling of that first love?" I threw at him, perhaps a bit hypocritically, as I had not succeeded in that myself.

"I have only been on the road a few years. You are much further along, but I must say that I am still having a wonderful time with God and am far from being bored with Him. I get the strong impression that the same is true the other way around. To summarize it biblically: There are no foxes in my vineyard yet, Pastor. The vineyard is still full of untouched flowering tendrils, the sun shines above it like never before, and the fencing around it looks like reinforced steel, if you ask me!"

With those words, Case put his finger on a sore spot without knowing it himself. Lydia glanced at me with a pained look and I quickly tried to change the subject of the conversation.

Indeed, that night before, Lydia and I had had a strong exchange of words about the letter from the board that had arrived. She demanded openness, but until I knew exactly what was going on, I decided to remain a closed book.

That letter did not come as a bolt from the blue to her. It was not the first time that I got into trouble in this area of my life, and if I would continue to refuse to wear my heart upon my sleeve, this would certainly not be the last time, according to her. It would be the last one Deborah would be involved in. She made that clear. The limit of seven times seventy came in sight.

Being divorced and a pastor, was the worst-case scenario for me. It is a bit like a lung doctor dying of lung cancer from frequent smoking. You are unable to put the solutions you provide to others into practice yourself.

Our early years were heavenly. We were as thick as thieves. Everything we undertook succeeded. Things went downhill after Peter was born. He was a darling little fellow, but also a crybaby. I once stood with him at the top of the stairs in the middle of a sleepless night and thought to my own horror: If I drop you now, there will be peace. But common sense, in that area at least, always won out over bouts of impulsiveness. He could not help it either.

I continued to serve the congregation during that time, as best I could, and Lydia, too, tried to keep her head above the water. But she repeatedly went under. She experienced one of the darkest periods in her life. She doubted she was a good mother, hesitated about her motherly feelings, and she felt guilty about all sorts of things for which she was not to blame.

Nowadays, you hear a lot about postpartum depression. But back then, mental problems were in the taboo area, especially for invincible Christians like us. He would surely make this all work out for the better, according to many well-meaning pieces of advice. She just had to choose joy over mourning, then everything would be like before. Just take back what the enemy stole! Those kinds of one-liners multiplied the guilt and gave it a vertical component.

Physical intimacy in those days was scarce, perfectly understandable, and legitimate in retrospect. But the toxic cocktail of public life as a pastor and the chaos of the young family behind the front door meant that the fences around our vineyard were brutally sabotaged. There were a few foxes gnawing and prying to create an opening. They hid during the day, but at night, out of our sight, they delivered their sneaky labor.

Our wedding text was Song of Songs 2:16: "My love is mine, and I am his." In hindsight, it is a mortal sin that no one pointed us to the verse that precedes: "Catch for us the foxes, the little foxes that ruin the vineyards, our vineyards that are in bloom."

Now these foxes look different in every marriage. What they all have in common is that they are sly and are not actually seen in daylight. A few years back, during a hiking retreat in Scotland, I saw one just during the day. I was sitting on a wooden bench, hidden under a canopy of leaves, and the little fox thought it could walk down the hill toward a riverbed undetected. It was unique and thus immediately the exception that proves the rule.

Female beauty has always been my fox. Let me be honest in that. Even after my own conversion, that has remained my weak spot. I have fasted, prayed, and taken vows. To no avail. It is as if that part of my being had difficulty being renewed, would not yield to the power of God's Spirit that took many other rooms of my heart without difficulty. It is as if you have assembled a whole team and are playing Premier League football, but you keep struggling with that central defender who joined from *Ball on the Roof 4* who has had it written into his multiyear contract that he must be in the starting eleven compulsorily. I do not know exactly what Paul's thorn in the flesh had been, but mine is crystal clear to me. I have played with many fires in my life, but this has always been the one I kept burning myself to.

Back then, it ended with a hiss. A little chatting, an occasional one-on-one meeting with a little too much and too long eye contact. The attention I no longer got at home I did get from what the Scriptures call a "strange woman." Yet it caused damage, even though there was never any "gross and intolerable sin" in people's eyes at the time. The damage occurred not in the church, but in our vineyard between me and my sweetheart. A piece was eaten away that has not yet grown properly. A wound that just will not heal, a broken bone that always remains susceptible to breaking again.

"Is it true, Martinus, what they write? Is it like what happened before? Who is it this time?" She bellowed at me that evening after reading the letter. "How do you keep doing this? Do you even know what you are risking? Your marriage, your relationship with the children, this home, your ministry! If it is true, I am gone, I do not care what they all think!"

I remained silent, as I often did. As a result, I rightly got the reproach thrown at my head as to why I could not just answer.

Our quarrels had become predictable by this time. Lydia had many words, but all of them ricocheted off the thick walls around my heart. I slumped down, staring through the window. All sorts of things lived in my heart at the time, but sharing it with another human being was impossible for me. Learned young is done old. Not learned is never done. This meant showing vulnerability, and that was a bridge too far for me. As if my emotions had been sentenced to life imprisonment somewhere in my own childhood.

Thinking about it now, I should have just opened my mouth, burst into tears. Opened up. After all, it was better for her to hear it from me than from somebody else. No left cheek, no second mile, no sheep to the slaughter without opening its mouth. Sometimes speaking is just gold and silence is silver. But I chose silver. It is a choice I regret to this day. What is done is done.

Case brought my thoughts back to the present with his signature laughter. "You know what I find so funny, Pastor? I sometimes secretly open my eyes at those altar calls and look over the congregation. Then I always hear the pastor say, "I saw your hand, I saw your hand too." Maybe he has the gift of hallucination, Martinus, but nobody is raising their hands! He sees things, which I do not see. Well, I reckon they register it correctly in the celestial chart box, don't you think, Mrs. Metgod?"

CHAPTER 4

TWO MEMORABLE WEEKENDS

On a Sunday evening in September of that memorable year, I received an email from our youth leader. An email on Sunday is often bad news, usually involving a voluminous comment, typed in red capital letters, about the content of my sermon. This time, fortunately, I was not the object of anyone's wrath.

The start-up weekend of teen work had just ended, and as agreed, I received a short message with feedback from Inge, our youth leader. It was to be Case's second public performance that season, after Thera and Tobias's wedding, and I was naturally curious to see if he had learned from his mistakes.

Someone talked me into preaching a message during this teen weekend. Do not get me wrong, youth work is important, period. But I felt hopelessly inadequate with such a group of bouncing hormones. Case had no problem taking over for me. Parents' reactions to that change of schedule could be divided into two categories. Category 1 was glad that their pastor was not coming along; after all, I might be suspected of indecent conduct with children or teenagers. Category 2 thought that I should go along anyway, since a pastor must have a feeling for all groups represented in the congregation. Anyway, I stayed home, and Case went. The report was entertaining; I am glad I kept it on file all these years.

* * *

Dear Brother Metgod,

As promised, you hereby receive the report of our youth group trip in which your intern, Case Parker, had the final say in things. We have just returned home from a noteworthy weekend. I reckon that you will be busy answering emails and calls all day tomorrow.

As the organizing committee, we had tasked Case with teaching our teens about rebirth. Call it miscommunication or a twist of fate, but this did not pan out.

In fact, Brother Case had sent the wrong PowerPoint to our tech team. During his talk, a presentation entitled "birth" instead of "rebirth" opened behind his back. Without him realizing it, what was being shown was not the bridge illustration and the transformation from caterpillar to butterfly, but the birth canal through which his niece saw the light of day in HD quality. I can tell you, Pastor, this caused quite a stir. The youngest teen group talked about this with their group leaders for a long time.

After everyone had calmed down again and coleader Esther had reassured the girls that not all births involve a total rupture and vacuum pump, it was time for the night game. This too was under Case's inspired leadership.

He had had the bright idea of playing glow-in-the-dark football, and to that end had bought two luminous balls from an obscure web store. "Inge, we'll let them play for five hours starting at two in the morning, we can sleep soundly!" I agreed and was ready for a good night of rest with everything going on at church.

As Case blew his whistle and kicked the ball into the teenage crowd, it suddenly dawned on me that while the ball might be luminous, this did not apply to the obstacles in the vicinity.

This created a surreal spectacle of a group of fifty invisible teenagers running frantically screaming after a luminous ball, but not just hitting the ball. With my night vision goggles, I saw heads hitting ancient oak trees, knees getting acquainted with concrete picnic benches, and the more noble parts of the body slamming hard against goal posts.

As the worst of the darkness passed, twilight made its appearance, and the game neared its end. The field behind the camp farm looked like a combined episode of MASH and ER. I watched a multitude that no one could count stumble bloodied across the field, some even without their front teeth.

In the end, most of the teeth were returned to their rightful owners, but I am sure many parents will be not amused when they get their offspring back tonight.

On behalf of all the youth leaders who were present this weekend, I would urge you not to be too hard on Case. He is genuinely nice company, and quite a few things went well. For example, he told a wonderful story about a fountain and a dump truck that brought the house down. Ask him about that story, will you? One-on-one, he managed to strike the right note with our teenagers. You want to hold on to this guy, believe me.

Well, I hope you can still laugh a little about it brother, you deserve that in these complicated times. Not everything said will be true, I estimate.

Love, Inge Zoetebier.

* * *

Looking back on it now, almost twenty years later, the report of this weekend was not too bad, compared to the weekend that Case would be preparing later that season.

As an internship assignment, he was responsible for planning and booking our church weekend out. After all, our congregation celebrated its twenty-five-year anniversary, and this had to be celebrated with a good old camping trip in early spring. March stirs its tail, we say in Holland; it wagged its tail extra that year, I can tell you that for sure.

Case had already told me that he is more a big picture kind of guy rather than filling in the details. That should have set off an alarm bell, but as we know, I had other issues to worry about at the time.

Proudly, he came to tell me that he had booked several hiker's huts, chalets, and pitches at a new Christian campground, somewhere on the other side of the province, called Eden. The contact with the owner was very pleasant, and the price was competitive, a plus for Dutch Christians, you will understand.

That church weekend is etched in many memories. What happens in Vegas, stays in Vegas. That applies to this weekend as well. Those who were present will look back on it with mixed feelings. It therefore seems better to not explain the details here, because there is a risk that you will then entrust these memoirs to the fireplace. In addition, several parishioners are still alive and that could cause a lot of pastoral misery! I can tell you this much: Campsite Eden used the pre-fall dress code, which came as a very unpleasant surprise to all of us!

It was weekends like this that led to many fires that I and the elders had to put out afterward. I was recently in Croatia and saw the word "pastor" on all the fire extinguishers there. Those guys in the Balkans understood perfectly well what kind of work I do.

At the same time, these events also gave luster to my suffering. It was weekends like these through which young Case made a name for himself and took his first shaky steps into the pastoral ministry. I do not just remember the mischief of this gentleman. For me, he will always remain the intern who did not mince words and through whom God could speak like no other.

CHAPTER 5

THE FOUNTAIN AND THE DUMP TRUCK

The days became shorter as fall arrived that year. Sr. Wierenga's Bridge club was working overtime and to combat the loneliness young Case stopped by more often in the evening for a good conversation.

"Maybe I'm wrong, Pastor, but two things struck me when I shared my testimony last week."

With a hand gesture, I invited him to expound on his thoughts.

He was not inhibited by a piece of apple pie with whipped cream because he continued talking, full-mouthed, while the whipped cream stuck between his nose and upper lip like a white mustache. "You were jealous of my first love, and when I started talking about the foxes in the vineyard, things got awkward between you and Mrs. Metgod. I may look like a mountain, Martinus, but these sensors here pick up all the signals." As he placed one hand on his heart to point out his sensors, he beckoned me with the same hand gesture to expound my thoughts. For a moment, the roles were reversed. The student became the mentor and the rabbi the follower.

"Your feelers are functioning fine, Case. I think you are right. I do not want to pour cold water on your fire, so we'd better let it rest. You will not understand it anyway, boy. These things are terribly complicated and take some life experience to grasp."

"Pastor, with all due respect, this is the umpteenth time you have said I will not understand. This can have two reasons. Either you think I am too young to soak up your life's wisdom like a sponge, or you would like to perpetuate the image you think I have of you. My uncle Vincent used to say that you can often learn more from a person's mistakes than from the things that unexpectedly went right. Now he is an alcoholic who, in addition, cannot stay away from other people's wives, but he certainly has a point in this area. Doesn't it also say in First Corinthians 10 that other people's stories act as examples and warnings for us? Well, spill the beans, Martinus. I would like to learn from your failures. You cannot take that chance away from me." With hands behind his head and legs wide, he dropped backwards into the chair. The thing almost collapsed. I decided to bring it home for him.

"That beautiful Golf VR6 of yours, Case. How long has that been your pride and joy?"

"I bought it just recently. Before that, I had a VW Golf Type II, my first little car."

"You must have been extremely happy with that when you bought it as your first car." A small nod in agreement. "But I bet at some point that car felt too ordinary, didn't it?"

"True Martinus, everything becomes dull and unattractive after a while, right?"

"Sure Case, everything does. Now I have a question for you: Was is that your Type II lost its appeal overnight or because you saw others driving a Golf VR6 with BBS rims and lowered chassis?" I was puzzled by my own jargon.

"I think the latter to be honest, Pastor."

"Well, that is in a nutshell what (has) happened to me in different areas. I will explain it to you so you can put your uncle Vincent's lesson into practice, boy. Like you, I really experienced such a moment of conversion. I fell, to speak with Acts, off my horse, and God healed me from my spiritual blindness and a sense of calling soon developed. Those first formative years were heavenly. Prayers were answered, conferences attended, I rededicated my life to Christ every day, my hand was always high up in the air.

"God did more than enough to let me know He could be trusted and was more real than the socks on my feet. He was like living water flowing through my backyard, my vineyard. Grassy meadows, calm waters. Case, it could not be beaten by anything this world has to offer.

"But gradually something changed. Not about Him, for that matter, but in my perception of Him and all He had to give. In my experience, the grass became yellowish and the water undrinkable. Instead of looking upward daily, I began to lurk around me. I began to think that I needed something more than Him alone, simply by focusing my eyes on what others, in my view, had and were.

"With my salary as a pastor, I could barely live from hand to mouth. The expensive holidays others took were a mission impossible for me. I became jealous of my neighbor who built beautiful houses for a living and closed his toolbox at four p.m. I started unconsciously blaming God that the Christian life apparently involved being incredibly busy with all sorts of things without getting anything in return. He was once my beloved Type II, but I began to long for the Golf VR6. Do you understand what I am saying, Case?"

"Certainly, Pastor. Not only do I understand it, but I already knew it."

With a puzzled look I looked at the lad. How could he know?

"The thing is, a while back, just before the youth camp, I dreamed about you Martinus. I reckon, as a Baptist, you will have to get used to the fact that God gives prophetic dreams to Drents singing the National Anthem at a funeral procession, but afterward you will thank me. Mrs. Metgod might too."

In the past, I had received some prophetic words, but that source seemed to have dried up. "I am all ears, Case. I would love to hear what you have seen and what you think it means. Who knows, maybe you are a bit like Joseph!" I told him, smiling, still not entirely convinced.

"I wrote it down for you, Pastor. In my teens, I drank so much that it has affected my memory. Take it and read." Case pressed his notebook into my hands. While browsing, I saw several lists of prayer points, dates with write-ups about what God had spoken. Short poems by his hand about God's holiness. On the last page described, I read his dream.

* * *

The fountain and the dump truck

Last night, God showed me a garden. It was a beautiful, enclosed garden. Everything seemed to be in bloom. Spring was getting ready to turn into summer. One flower was even brighter in color than another, and in the trees nested various kinds of birds that found shelter under the dozens of shades of green of the thick leaves.

God told me it was okay to open the gate to enter, even if it was someone else's garden. For a fleeting time, I walked along the paths, enjoying with all my senses everything I saw, felt, heard, and smelled. A beautiful thick oak tree, the tapping of a pied woodpecker, the sun sparkling the dew, and sound and sight of the streams of water made it like heaven on earth.

The path I walked ended at what must have been the center of the garden. All paths seemed to end there. There, at the middle, was a beautiful ornate fountain, twenty meters in diameter. Powerful too. With great intensity, the water spewed through the underground pipes and flowed through an ornamental ornament to the four lower water plateaus. Once on the ground, it flowed into several branches of the river I had just seen.

I sat down on a wooden bench at the edge of a meadow and looked at the water that supplied the whole garden with life bringing water.

This peaceful scene was interrupted by a swelling sound from outside the estate. It came closer, and I heard twigs crunching under what sounded like car tires. I saw a few animals sprinting away and bathing birds making their escape. On the path, indeed, I saw a car with a small trailer approaching. Two men stoically got out and grabbed a shovel from their trunk. When I got up, I saw that there was yellow sand in the trailer. The men began scooping out the sand and throwing it into the fountain and its branches.

I wanted to get up to have a heart-to-heart with them, but a hand pushed me back onto the wooden bench and constrained me so I could not move left or right. I tried with everything in me to stop them, but I was fighting a losing battle. A voice spoke, "Case, stay seated and learn from what you are about to see."

The next moment I saw years flash by me. I saw a tear-off calendar from which the ever-darkening pages were rapidly fading with ever-changing years. I saw the trees growing, losing leaves, and gaining new ones. The sun was sometimes high, sometimes low. The garden was sometimes green, then autumnal yellow or wintry white. Nests were full of young birds and later empty again.

God pointed out a striking scene to me. As time went on and the years passed, more cars came to the fountain to drop sand in its basin. The cars grew larger as time passed and the trailers also grew longer. The cars became vans, the vans became agricultural vehicles, which in turn were replaced by dump trucks. Two men became four, eight, dozens.

As I sat chained to the bench, I watched them dump more sand into the fountain before leaving again. Their large vehicles made deep tracks in the forest. Before, the fountain shot meters high into the air, but now there was nothing more to see. The sand became too heavy, the water pressure insufficient, the water stopped flowing. No longer did it stream into the river with its branches. The once green garden turned yellowish, the birds no longer built their nests, and the creeks ran dry.

When I was loosened again and walked to the exit, the garden looked nothing like how it looked when I entered. I looked back once more, angry and disappointed after I walked out of the gate. The gate was closed. Written in cast iron letters was: Welcome to the Garden of Faded Glory.

"The voice told me to write down what I had seen and let you read it, Martinus. I have a notepad next to my bed so I cannot forget. I'll tell you what I think it means and then you have to say whether I understand, or if I am indeed too young and inexperienced, okay?"

I was shaken to the core and invited him to explain the dream. "It is like this, Pastor. The first years after your conversion and of your married life were like how the garden once was. Everything you touched turned to gold, everything you undertook succeeded. You had short lines of communication with God and walked abundantly with Him. You and Lydia had a good time together. The fountain splashed high, and the water reached deep into the garden through its various branches. Everything in your life was blooming. You were content, satiated in every area.

"But gradually you started slacking off. You allowed things into your garden that should not be there at all. At first, they drove around the edge of the garden, but at some point, you opened the gate, and they managed to reach the epicenter of your being, your fountain. You let them throw sand into your engine, throw plastic soup into your ocean, dump contaminated soil into your fountain.

"Then you came to a tipping point. At the beginning, you thought it would be no big deal. Everybody out there had times that they did not read their Bible for a week. A shepherd is only a sheep too, right? Besides, of course, nothing human or mannish is foreign to you. You have deluded yourself into thinking that looking at another woman is no problem if it stops there.

"What you did not realize is that by doing so, you opened the gate wider and wider. Sin always wants more, Pastor. It is never satisfied, is always hungry. To achieve the same effect, you needed more of that which destroyed you from the inside out. The cars got bigger and their visits to your fountain more frequent. To be direct, Pastor: I think over the years you have slowly let the fire of the Holy Spirit die out. You have not taken very good care of your fountain, so everything in you and around you is slowly losing their luster and dying."

I had to admit to young Case that he understood more about it than I had thought. In fact, he may have understood more of it than I did. He went down in history as the first student I have had under my care who received prophetic dreams that made sense. I knew it was a direct word from God to me.

Case confided in me that it was not too late; the glory had not yet completely departed. It did not have to end the way it did in the dream. Yet it felt different. I was caught between a rock and a hard place and had not a single clue how to get out.

CHAPTER 6

THE INCIDENT AND THE DEFENSE

The letter from the investigating committee, on behalf of the board, naturally invited a reply. Following good practice, I was given several weeks to draft my rebuttal. Countless times I sat at the kitchen table with a black coffee, writing paper, and my favorite pen, waiting for words to appear on the paper. But they did not. Where to start, with the truth or pulling the wool over their eyes? With apologies or a rundown of the situation? Or simply with a few clarifying questions?

Officially, it was still a mystery as to exactly which boundaries I had crossed. Unofficially, I knew full well what this was about. I examined myself, holding my pen just inches above the pristine white of the writing paper. Had I repented of what had occurred or regretted the consequences? That makes quite a difference.

I remember once, in a game of bow and arrow, our Peter had shot an older neighbor boy right between the eyes with a wooden arrow that got stuck in his skull. The poor boy ran, arrow and all, right through our conifer hedge and rhododendrons toward his parents' house where Mother managed to pull the arrow out of his head. Peter was out of his mind, frightened. We had to punish him. As it turned out, he was not even particularly sorry that he had almost killed his neighbor, but was sad because he was not allowed to watch any episodes of *A-Team* all week as punishment for his Robin Hood act.

To be honest, at the time, I too was particularly angered by the consequences and not so much by the incident itself. The gossip, not being allowed to perform certain tasks in my ministry, it was all hopelessly complicated. The tension at home, the awkward silences between me and Lydia, super irritating. What had happened was just a storm in a teacup, humanly speaking. Although I do not know exactly what Saskia made of it when she confided in the elders without consulting me first.

Saskia was a vulnerable woman, just divorced from a man who mentally and physically abused her. These days, any man who takes leadership is labeled a narcissist at home and at work, but Saskia's ex had the diagnosis.

She had been assigned accelerated, emergency housing around the corner from the church. She attended the service, and at the exit I shook hands with her as I did with all church members to wish them a good week, hoping to catch a few more compliments on the sermon as well. She was at the back of the line, and we lingered for a while. She told me in a nutshell how her life had gone so far. I asked her if she would like to talk a little longer, and she was up for that. She hardly knew anyone in the neighborhood yet, and companionship and a heart-to-heart conversation was a fine prospect.

Together with a female volunteer within our pastoral team, I met with her for a year. Mostly at church, sometimes at her home. She told her story, gained strength, and regained her faith from days of old. She had a voice like gold and soon started singing along with our praise combo, a hip name at the time for

Baptists who had access to four chords and a large dose of self-confidence, if you ask me. Every now and then she would be scheduled in as worship leader, and we would start meeting one-on-one to prepare the church services. She often picked out beautiful songs to go with the themes I was preaching on. I thanked God that she had fallen into our lap, my lap.

I noticed that in her presence, Lydia's mental swings had less impact on me. They disappeared like snow in the sun; it seemed. That first postpartum depression was not isolated. She also turned ill after Elizabeth's birth. There was often a lack of understanding. A broken leg stands out; a broken spirit does not. I, too, sometimes found it difficult to understand her mood swings. There was separation, the foxes became visible even during the daytime. No longer were we equals. I sometimes regarded her as inferior, unstable, weak. In my worst moments, I expressed this verbally, often during one of our fights. It was not all doom and gloom, though. Repeatedly Lydia drew strength from somewhere to climb back out of the valley, but the swings were always lurking.

Saskia and I laughed a bit back in the day. When I came home, after a run-through of that week's service, I was often cheerful, which did not escape Lydia either: "If Saskia had had one leg, weighed 200 kilos, and had a big pimple on her nose it probably wouldn't have been as much fun, would it, Martinus?" I then looked momentarily aggrieved, as if she were the Pharisee and I were the true follower. She, Martha, who worried about many things, and I, Lazarus, who had risen renewed from his grave. I understood very well what she meant; she certainly had a point though I would never admit it.

Before the incident, which I still feel was making a mountain out of a molehill, Saskia and I had threaded through the eye of the needle a few times. A few flattering text messages back and forth, a little too much eye contact, three kisses on the cheeks when it was her birthday where things got awkward for a moment because there was no one else in the room but the two of us.

Thursday, June 12, 2004, was one of those days that, in retrospect, I would rather not have gotten up out of bed. It was raining cats and dogs, and summer still seemed far away. The night before, I had an elders' meeting that had ended just before midnight. One of the children had the stomach flu and Lydia had just complained again, before the clock struck eight, about the imbalance between my work and private life. She had seen in my diary that I had an appointment with Saskia that morning and that did not improve the atmosphere. I left in anger, slamming doors and heading for the church, where I dropped down in my office chair around ten. Saskia had been so good to get two delicious cappuccinos from that new coffee shop down the road.

The reason for our being together was the ending of a long pastoral journey. This trajectory began with three of us, but would end today with two of us. Saskia experienced a deeper connection with me than with the female volunteer, and she became the exception that proves the rule. I had sworn on all and sundry that I would never have pastoral and confidential conversations with a woman alone. I was aware of my thorn in the flesh, and if I forgot, I had an excellent assistant in Lydia to remind me. In this case, I turned out to be a little less principled than I pretended to be toward colleagues. Meeting her by myself was like pulling the pin from a grenade.

That morning, she told me again about the horrors her ex-husband had done to her. She was crying, vulnerable, and attractive. My sense of justice came on strong. With the pitiful state of my marriage, at least that is what I had made of it in the back of my mind, as a backdrop, I decided to get up and walk over to Saskia who was sitting on the other side of the table. She stood and, for a moment, I looked into her green eyes and kissed her on her forehead. I then pressed her against me for just a second before stepping back and complimenting her on her openness.

I realized that I had just taken several dangerous steps toward the wild waters of the ocean and its foam-headed waves. The deep sea was calling me by name. Saskia seemed shocked, put her handkerchief away in her purse and left headlong with an excuse that she had an appointment with the owner of her rental property that was struggling with several leaks. I was like Potiphar's wife, she like Joseph. Had I gone too far? Did I cross the line?

I stayed in the office for a while and then headed home for lunch. I was struggling to make it through the day and could not do any form of meaningful work. Nothing crazy had happened, had it? My in-house lawyer argued lustily, trying to downplay the meaningless kiss, with little success, for that matter.

I was heading downhill for disaster and on the verge of throwing away everything I had built up in the first half of my life. When you are angry, there is always a plate to throw. When you want to be away from God, there is always a boat to take you to faraway places, just like with Jonah. Saskia was just the right person in the wrong place, or the other way around. Something in me wanted to meet up with her again soon. How had she experienced it? Why had she run away so quickly? Was I falling in love with her, or she with me? What would it be like to...

* * *

Dear Brothers of the Board,

I have received your letter indicating that you are suspending me pending the investigation. I see it as the first stone thrown by people who themselves have never known sin. It would have been nice if you would have disclosed what, in your humble opinion, took place. Surely you must also know that I am not just any preacher. I deserve more than this. It is hard to defend yourself when you do not know what you are accused of, isn't it?

What always amazes me in issues like this is that, from the board, no one has ever been reprimanded for a proud look or a lying tongue, a heart that devises wickedness or sowing discord among brethren. Some of these things are an abomination to the Lord we read in the Word, but you are using a different top five than the list hanging on the heavenly bulletin boards. But rest assured, you are in good company: I have never lovingly put anyone under discipline because of hidden sin. I have since come to the conviction that I have such an incredibly large plank in my own eye that it is therefore almost impossible to spot the speck in someone else's. I am glad that our denomination is clearly led by men who have removed their own logs and thrown them into the fire so that they can sort poor wretches like Martinus here, out. Where would we be without you up there in your ivory tower, right?

Let me tell you another fun thing. Several years ago, I participated in a fifty-kilometer step race to raise funds for the re-evangelization of our continent. I had not trained, but I had tremendous confidence in my own ability. This resulted in quite a fall after only two kilometers of stepping. Blood poured out of my knee, and my running shorts showed a tear and soon turned dark red.

However, I had luck on my side; no one had seen my fall. The group in front of me was too far away, and I had shaken off the rear guard. The same luck unfortunately did not fall to my colleague Kees. He, too, fell but did so amid the modest peloton. He got the laughs, a pat on the shoulder and continued his way. Both of us finished seven hours later after fifty long kilometers. Both of us had fallen, but that fall of mine had never come to light you see. Back to today: My fall is now in the view of many, but I am genuinely curious about your own falls. Perhaps you have fallen on a different road than I have, and your fall has been covered with the cloak of charity, but falling is falling right?

Having said that, I must confess that it is good for me to be forced to eat humble pie; it might put a stop to my inner considerations. After all, man is not unclean because of what enters his mouth, but because of what lives inside. Perhaps this is God's way of keeping me from worse things. Who knows? It will not be the first time His ways have proved unfathomable.

I saw your thrown stone fly and caught it, only there was nothing written on it. So, men, spit it out. I would like to hear the charges so I can properly defend myself. It could just be that this will all end with a hissy fit, and that would benefit all parties, including my Lydia, I think.

A brotherly greeting,
Pastor Martinus Metgod.

* * *

When I made Case read my letter, he found it defensive in nature, yet I stuck the stamp and put it in the mailbox, relieved, combative, and a tad recalcitrant. The higher-ups of our denomination had just started barking up the wrong tree. They were going to find out tomorrow when they would read the letter and be shaken to their core.

Less than two days later, I received a phone call from the chairperson of the board. Lydia switched the phone to my study, after which I had a surreal conversation with this bearer of bad news. Lydia had sat in my easy chair on the other side of the room and demanded to listen in via speakerphone so she would hear firsthand what I was charged with, and I would have no chance to beat around the bush.

That conversation aggravated the agony. Although I defended valiantly, the suspicion was enough to put me at 0-5 down, playing with ten men and three minutes to go and my laces untied. It was a hammer blow. The home crowd started waving their white handkerchiefs, the rest were looking for the exit before the final whistle. I was facing my own mission impossible, and Tom Cruise was nowhere to be seen.

Attempted sexual assault. Those three words echoed between the four walls of my home office like a tennis serve at an indoor match. The window stills of the single glass were springing up. On the twelfth of June, in the morning, I had attempted to assault Saskia sexually in my office, in church, during a pastoral meeting, the chair disclosed.

When those words were spoken, I looked in surprise, slightly blushing, at my easy chair. There sat Lydia. Silent, trembling lower lip, pale. As if all the life had just been sucked out of her. As if she had just heard that Peter and Elizabeth had died in a traffic accident. No support. No hand on my shoulder because she could not believe it. No, acceptance, as if she had known all along. No thunder from a clear blue sky. At most, a small sigh of wind on a profoundly wet and gray autumn day, nothing to be surprised about.

While stammering, I stuttered that I thought this allegation was over the top and tried to explain what, in my increasingly modest opinion, had happened that day. The conclusion of a pastoral journey indeed, the kiss on the forehead and Saskia's unexpectedly quick departure. Perhaps this had brought something from her past to the surface and caused her to perceive it differently, I told them, but I couldn't be held responsible for that, could I? Surely there was not that much going on? So much fuss over one kiss on a forehead? I had been blameless all these years, hadn't I? Surely an immaculate record, decades long, is worth much more than the interpretation of one vulnerable church member about an isolated incident one Thursday morning?

When I put down the handset because I noticed I was making no progress, the other chair was empty and the door closed. I was alone, abandoned, framed, misunderstood. It already felt a lot less nice to be eating humble pie. Everything has a beginning; many things also have an end. Was this the beginning of the end?

Chapter 7

Two Baskets Full of Fruit

After the disastrous phone call, the words "attempted sexual assault" echoed through our almost empty house for days to come. Lydia had stormed off furiously and told the children that Grandpa and Grandma had invited the three of them to come and stay for a few nights. I gave Peter and Elizabeth a kiss and tried to do the same to Lydia, while she only had eyes for the kids who she strapped in their car seats. I wished them a nice sleepover as if there was a cut-and-paste function in life that would allow me to erase the board's little phone call at the touch of a button.

Lydia had barely left when I received a text message. Saskia. Whether she could come over for a chat. In her own words, she was shocked by the consequences of her report, was eager to make amends and closed with a "Love, Saskia." The timing could not have been worse or better?

Once Lydia and I were shopping during our engagement period. I am one of those guys who waits outside the shop while my wife strolls through the clothing racks under pressure.

As we toured from store to store, I succeeded to stand in

dog poop, much to Lydia's hilarity. I decided, like a small child, to walk away angrily and take the train home instead of the car that was parked in the downtown parking lot. In a narrow alley towards the central station, I bumped into Hanna. A girl from our student union who, together with Lydia, had tried to lay claim to my affection and had come out on the losing end.

We struck up a conversation, talked about old times, and she invited me to her house for coffee. Fortunately, I had the presence of mind to recognize this as one of the seducer's dirty tactics. I angrily continued my walk toward the station, only to turn around halfway so as not to wander off completely. Lydia was still standing at the scene. As if she knew I could not do without her.

In all honesty, I was dying to see Saskia that night. To hear her side of the story, to talk to her for a while. Just to spend some time together.

I texted back that tonight was not the best fit, but that I would get back to her soon. I hesitated for a moment whether, in turn, I should add a "Love, Martinus" to that as well. I tapped the letters and stared at my screen for a moment but decided to erase them and just make it an old-fashioned "Heartfelt Greetings" as I did with other church members.

There was going to be another evening of Bridge that night, so I decided to invite Case to my house for some distraction and provide him with the latest intel. Before long, I heard the Volkswagen drive into the yard. I had asked him to bring two pints of canned Guinness to keep us company.

"Welcome boy, first I am going to teach you how to drink a glass of Guinness. Not all worldly things are foreign to me, but you already know that by now." I asked him to grab from the top kitchen cabinet above the sink two large Guinness glasses I once bought on a tour of the Guinness factory in Dublin.

"Watch and listen, boy. You open the can and leave it for a moment."

Case did as I said, opening cans of beer was not new to him of course. "Now you take the glass and hold it at an angle of about forty-five degrees and let three quarters slowly flow into the glass." Case was once again flawless. "Are you ready for the final?" With a nod, he indicated he could not wait. "Now you pour the last quarter while it is on the table, which will cause a small head of foam to form." Just like that. "Good boy, now you do the same thing again with mine and then we will wait a minute before this wheat smoothie turns from dark brown to black and then we are ready to drink."

While Case perfected his craft, I grabbed a large bag of M&M's and stoked up the fireplace. Ready for an enjoyable conversation and a hearty confession.

"Say Pastor, it's awfully quiet here at home. Maybe you should shower more often, that will keep them in for sure."

"Yes, boy, Lydia and the kids left, and I suspect it is a one-way trip." With a cold glass of Guinness in his hand, he invited me to clarify their absence. "I got a call this afternoon Case. Attempted sexual assault is what they have charged me with. Be watchful, you are drinking alcohol here with a sexual predator. This could well go wrong." I had managed to suppress my sarcasm of old, but now under the burden of pastoral termination, it began to rear its nasty head again.

"That's serious stuff, Martinus. Apparently it didn't work out?"

"What do you mean, Case?"

"Well, it was only an attempt, but I must say I find that is bad enough, Martinus. In a pub in Drenthe, you should not have risked that with one of our girls."

I decided to recount what had taken place in June with all

its gory details to disprove that I was some dirty little man looking prowling for a vulnerable female victim.

He was silent for a moment and took another sip and a handful of M&M's. "Tell me this. Will this ordeal haunt you later at the final judgment, Martinus? Do you think God will have a heart to heart with you about what happened later?"

"Well, Case, in Micah, it says that He has thrown our sins into the depths of the sea. Corrie ten Boom once said that He also put a sign next to it: 'Fishing prohibited.' When you look at it that way, I estimate that He already knew this was going to happen and that in Christ He has forgiven me, but to be honest, it does not feel that way right now. Here in an empty house, wife and kids gone and a big sword of Damocles hanging over my position as pastor, my confidence is shrinking a bit. I cannot deny there probably is a fair amount of disappointment in heaven over what I have done."

"Do you know what I think, Martinus? I think that things could go very differently on that judgment day than you feel right now. You will not be surprised after that dream about the fountain and the garden, but I strongly suspect that God has shown me what judgment will look like for us Baptists later. I got an inside look, and it is incredibly similar to what I find in the Bible. Are you ready for some teaching on this sad day, Pastor?"

I beckoned along the lines of "come on" and took a big swig of the black gold myself.

"I worked behind the scenes at a greengrocer for a while and was responsible, among other things, for separating rotten and healthy fruit. Early in the morning, the chief would come with big baskets of vegetables, and it was up to me to pick out the rotten apples. When I was doing that one Saturday morning, I suddenly understood the judgment on believers, and I include Baptists in that too.

"Look, Pastor, when you close your eyes here for the last time on this side of eternity, then you may go straight into rest. No more difficult conversations, no more arguing with Lydia, no more temptations; it is finished immediately. Sometime later in time, you, too, will be allowed to appear before the judgment seat of Christ to see what has gone well and not so well. Not to be condemned, Pastor, because as you yourself have preached countless times to others, there is no more condemnation for those who are in Christ. The measure of reward will then take center stage on that day. Are you still following me?" He grabbed two wicker baskets from the windowsill and a handful of kiwis from the fruit bowl and sat back down.

"These kiwis symbolize for a moment all the fruit you have borne in your long life as a stumbling follower and imperfect pastor. They consist of the visible things you have done for us, your family, the congregation but also for the deliberations and intentions of your heart; that which was not visible to anyone, only to Him and partly to yourself. On that momentous day, your works and fruits will be under the magnifying glass, and it will become clear whether they were as ripe as you and others thought or were rotten inside after all.

"Looks can deceive, Pastor. Sometimes customers returned apples that looked fine on the outside, but after a cross-section were completely rotten. That cross-section will happen in heaven. We cannot do that. It is Jesus Himself who is going to take your fruit and put it in the two different baskets. Ripe and beautiful or rotten and unusable. All those rotten fruits of yours, as well as mine, are eventually transferred to an exceptionally large cross-shaped wicker basket with a text above it, 'For this I died.' They are finely pressed, disposed of, disappear into the pond of oblivion where Corrie's sign above it reads, 'Forbidden to eat and touch.'

"What remains is all the beauty that you, too, Martinus, have done for Him. On that basis, you, too, will receive a reward and may enter even more peace, golden streets, and things like that."

I looked at the Drent and realized that the Most High was once again using the foolishness of this world to shame this wayward pastor. But the lesson was not yet over.

With another handful of M&M's, he walked from the kitchen to my study. I heard him rummaging in the bookcase, and he returned with two copies. "Should you still not grasp it by now, Pastor, we'll apply the power of repetition to hit home the message." He sat down again and laid two books open on the table.

"Just imagine for a moment the following. Up there with God are countless bookshelves. Unlike most clergy who buy them to appear knowledgeable, the books are all known to Him and read by Him. When you have gone the way of all the earth, your books will be opened too, Pastor. That book is full of loose pages. All your works and your motives are neatly written on it. The tip of the iceberg that was visible to everyone, but also the foot that has been hiding in the dark and deep water all this time. Right in front of you, two stacks of it. A stack of failing grades and a pile of works that passed the time just fine.

"You will begin to see that a second book is then opened titled *The Book of Life*. I am not sure if it is in alphabetical order, Martinus, but there will be no doubt that Jesus will know how to locate your name in that book at lightning speed. Because your name is found in it, He will take two matches and place them in the shape of a cross under your stack of imperfections. He will draw you close to himself and say to you, 'For this I died.' Then He will light both matches and you will watch them burn up together. Who knows, there will be a sign,

'Forbidden to extinguish'. Together you will go back to that other stack and, based on that, you will receive a reward, Martinus. Well, let those theological wheels of yours turn and you tell me if I am about right here."

My mother used to say that when there was drink in the man, wisdom remained in the can, but with young Case that could not be said. The wisdom and deep thinking had not lost its sharpness even through more than half a pint of Guinness.

"What I want you to understand, Martinus. All is not lost; you cannot hit a home run all the time. Be kind to yourself. You are making a mess of things right now, but it does not have to end like this. Better times are sure to come for you too. Like those American preachers always say: Your best days are still in front of you. Maybe Lydia and the rascals will just come back after a cooling-off period."

"Preaching grace and living on grace yourself are two different things, Case. I hope you can always see it the way you tell it now, boy, which would make you an incredibly pleasant person and pastor."

"Just out of curiosity, Pastor, did you deliberately bring a rodent into your home that you let roam freely?"

Surprised by the change of subject, I shook no.

"Well, there is one over there on the kitchen counter moving towards your whole wheat bread."

Living in an old parsonage is very pleasant. I always enjoyed the atmosphere and the authentic elements, but so did the mice. By now they were used to my traps and were able to eat the cheese and chocolate spread without killing themselves like their ancestors in earlier years.

"Luckily Lydia is gone. She would go completely crazy! I will go catch it. You can take it to Sr. Wierenga. Seems like an animal lover too." Upon closer inspection of the little critter, I began to wonder whether this was a mouse or something else.

Neither Case nor I could figure it out and we decided to place the little one in a shoebox with breathing holes in it, under the stairs, to study it more closely the next day. We gave each other an awkward hug, with some slaps on the back as Case left. His were so hard I almost coughed up blood, but he meant well. The Bible says that some people have hosted angels without knowing it themselves. I began to think that Case might be one.

Early the next day, he was back to find out what kind of animal we had put in the shoebox. "Martinus, I am afraid the patient died. It may have been the draft or perhaps he was claustrophobic." The animal was curled up in the box with eyes squinted and indeed showed no sign of life. Case grabbed it by the tail and let it swing back and forth like a pendulum, hoping it would wake up, but those hopes proved vain.

"It is what it is, just throw it in the bin, will you? It is at the back, just in front of the back window. As compost, it might be of some use to me."

Case opted for a burial at sea, but since the pipes were not of the thicker kind, I had to convince him that I did not want to call a plumber. We threw the little one in the bin. Good riddance. You cannot mess with Martinus and his interns! We had a cup of coffee and filled out some evaluation forms for his internship as we chatted some more about the judgment of the faithful.

A few hours later, someone knocked on the door. I ran into the hallway, secretly hoping it was Lydia with both children. It turned out to be a concerned neighbor along with her daughter. The child seemed heartbroken. She sobbed and said she was looking for her little hamster that had disappeared without a trace the day before. The fluffy little animal, according to mother, tended to expand its territory and had already escaped their attention and its own cage several times to explore the wide world.

The girl only just managed to say that she felt so stupid not to have closed its playhouse properly, and now little Dixie was gone. The girl showed a picture of the creature on Mom's phone and at the sight of it; I was shocked. The beloved creature looked eerily like the one that tried to steal my daily bread yesterday and had been expertly recycled by Case just hours ago.

I decided to ask a handful of explanatory questions to save myself some time and suddenly realized that hamsters not only lie deathly still when they are dead but also when they start hibernating.

I decided to call Case to keep the unexpected visitor busy at the door with the excuse that I had chicken breast on the stove and did not want to burn it. When Case went to his knees to comfort the child, I made my way outside to open the bin to check if the beast was dead or still alive.

In turn, Case did exactly what he should not have done. He extended biblical hospitality by inviting mother and child to come in for a cup of tea. As they sat down on the couch, Mother looked out the window, startled. She saw me hanging forward in the wheelie bin.

When I came back up, she saw me triumphantly holding up a small animal, covered in dust and dirt (I had cleaned the fireplace last night before I went to bed), by its ears between my thumb and forefinger. With a few firm taps against its bulging cheeks, I tried to discover whether the creature had really walked into the eternal hamster heavens or had unsuspectingly gone to sleep in a shoebox under my stairs.

When I reentered the house after a few minutes with the hyperventilating hamster in my left hand, the neighbor girl's joy was complete. Avoiding the mother's piercing eyes, I decided to encourage the happy child with the observation that if we search long and earnestly, we will eventually find. "What is true of salvation is also true of hamsters, young lady," I reassured her.

When I heard from Case that Mother had watched the whole event with thunder in her eyes, I wondered if the spiritual lesson I was imparting to the child would fall on good soil.

CHAPTER 8

THE BRIDAL STORE

You cannot judge a guy like Case Parker solely on his public activities. Fortunately, because the beginning was all tempestuous, as described above. I was therefore delighted that Sr. Wierenga was willing to commit her findings to paper. She was a widow, a tall figure with a distinguished record in business development. A champion of feminism. Not the type I found easy to have a good relationship with. We had to get used to each other those first years, and I am expressing myself mildly.

At the same time, I got to know her as someone with a heart of gold, and someone who could read people to perfection and yet refrain from passing judgment. After the death of her husband, Evert, she made a guest room available to the trainees I supervised. It was like clockwork; after the first quarter, she entrusted me with her handwritten observations on every one of them. I enjoyed her perceptiveness, her humor. Between the perfectly written lines I regularly recognized what I saw myself, but sometimes her observations surprised me too.

Let me put it this way; together we discovered that many young gentlemen lived like a twenty-first-century version of Jekyll and Hyde. Pleasant in the pulpit and in the public life, but much less pleasant in private. They knew how to go with the flow in public, but privately, there was often little of the reality they preached. I never saw that as a problem. In those early developmental years, there is still plenty of time for balance between the two.

Case was a pleasant exception; he was the salt of the earth; he practiced what he preached. Congruent, as Sr. Wierenga would describe it, were she alive today.

* * *

Dear Martinus,

When I arrived home last night, after a fine St. Nicholas celebration with the children and grandchildren, it occurred to me that I had not yet written to you about the gentleman who has been calling my residence his home for more than three months. I enjoy being your extra pair of eyes, and I think you will sit back satisfied when you archive this letter after reading it.

My granddaughter was present at the youth camp, and my son-in-law walked in the funeral procession that you brightened up with your childish behavior. Both were touched. My grandchild by the beautiful story Case shared, her father by Case's unique talent for being able to make a joke out of everything.

Martinus, Case is a young man with two faces. But not in a negative way. You can overlap these faces, as it were, and what you see is satisfying. They are both sides of the coin, united, consistent, in harmony. I will outline both.

First, there is something childlike in this boy. Some will call it immature or impulsive; I call it authentic, playful. He seems free of any straitjacket. He explores, keeps the good, and can laugh at that which he eventually throws away without experiencing a shred of guilt about it. As if this part of him was born before the fall. As if he is frolicking in the evening chill, hand in hand with the Creator of all that lives.

I told you about the long-running conflict with my neighbor Arend, right? He is an old humbug, as bitter as an unroasted almond. Stingy, too; the dues for the neighborhood association always must be dragged out in front of hell's gates. Evert used to say that Arend is so frugal that he cries with one eye to spare his other tear duct.

When I told Case of my trouble with Arend, he thought it would be fun to play a joke on him.

Arend usually sits in front of the TV all evening, and I know his favorite program is Kassa, *with that charming Felix Meurders as host. Case decided to put him through his paces. He went to Blokker store and bought a universal remote control. On the evening that* Kassa *was broadcasted, he snuck outside and hid behind the conifer hedge positioned by Arend about three meters in front of the front window so as not to give curious passersby a glimpse of his TV behavior. Curtains are too expensive, need washing, and are see-through. In a half-hour speech, he had already confided to Evert that conifers could live up to a thousand years, value for money.*

In his calculations, however, Arend had not considered the infrared light from a remote control combined with a Drent's unbridled imagination.

One evening, Case gently snuck through the shrubbery like an accomplished commando. Through the overgrowth, he could see Arend sitting with a glass of water and a dry baby biscuit, feet stretched out on his faux leather couch. When the opening tune of Kassa *sounded, Case pressed his universal remote, which had no trouble with the conifer hedge and Arend's triple glazing. The TV jumped to the music channel MTV where Marco Borsato and Ali B were performing the song "What Would You Do?" live to a packed football stadium in Rotterdam.*

Arend got up slightly irritated, grabbed his own device and zapped back to Channel 1 and lay back down. Case rushed inside and shouted that I really should get out and join in on all the fun. He grabbed a plastic garden chair and exhorted me to sit behind the conifer hedge and occasionally raise the volume and operate the other buttons to change the channels.

Martinus, I do not know if I must account for this at the final judgment, but it was an evening never to be forgotten. Together we drove poor Arend to madness. In fact, it was so bad that the next day he had no trouble rolling over his money to get a new TV!

I remember when Evert and I were appointed as elders that you then talked about the qualities an elder should possess. What has always stayed with me in that is that he should be well known to outsiders as well, above reproach you called it. I do not know if the same conditions apply to trainees, but with Case there can be some skeletons coming out of the closet in that area. He is a real rascal; some background checks in Drenthe and the surrounding provinces seem a bare necessity before he moves into his first position as pastor!

Well, Sr. Wierenga confirmed the light-hearted and humorous side of the Drent. I estimated that Evert would have done everything not to miss this evening, fine brother he was. I could always be myself with him. What followed also confirmed the other side of the coin. It was not all roses.

Trust me, Martinus, there is also another side to this man. You know that I sometimes disagree with you profoundly with your tendency to always leave everything as it is. Evert and I have often tried to persuade you to apply the methods of that nice Mr. Bill Hybels in our church. His "seeker friendly" approach to church planting is now widely used and a remarkable success. In any case, God has bestowed His blessing to it because not only the churches in America are growing, but also some in the

Netherlands are flourishing because of his approach to church government.

I must honestly confess to you, Martinus, that I tried to pull young Case onto my team last week, hoping he could speak some sense into you. I had him listening to a sermon by Brother Hybels and read a book on his methodology, hoping that he would succeed where Evert and I failed. I had gained considerable steam and thought I had him where I wanted him. But one story from him was enough to shut me up, and you know Martinus that is not easy to do!

You know that I sometimes worry about Case, a bit like a grandmother does about her grandchild. Grandparents stand at a distance, but for that very reason sometimes see things more clearly than parents do. Especially at night, I sometimes hold my breath. In the dark, worries are often greater than during the day, of course.

Our bedrooms border, and I hear things there that I have never heard before. In the dead of night there are regular painful moans, hurried whispers, and soft cries. Once it was so bad that I did not trust it and sneaked out to check. Case was lying in his bed, but it was like he was battling an invisible enemy. He was out of breath, sweating, and speaking gibberish. I decided to dab his forehead with a washcloth and tuck him in as I did with Evert when the illness took over those last days before his pilgrimage ended. Case was so out of it that night that he did not even realize I was in his bedroom.

What amazes me is that, after these episodes, he wakes up early in the morning as if nothing happened. He sits down at the table, takes a black coffee and a sandwich, and sits down to write as if his life depended on it. The rest of the day he is his cheerful and friendly self.

Anyway, when I again, a little too early for him on the day, praised Mr. Hybels, he asked me to sit down. He asked me to *hand him his notebook. That night he had received a dream, and he thought it would be interesting for me to read the outline of it. Now I did not ask permission to share this with you, Martinus, but sometimes it is better to ask forgiveness afterwards than permission beforehand, right? Here then is Case's dream:*

I woke up in the dead hours of the night, in a panic, unable to get back to sleep. In my dream I saw a shop window full of beautiful white wedding clothes. I saw a man carefully fitting the mannequins with the most beautiful white dresses and long veils. No extravaganza in design, just beautiful long dresses that completely covered the bride from her neck to her toes. I could already envisage the bride shining on what would undoubtedly be one of the most beautiful days of her life.

The man left the shop window and spoke words to his staff that obviously saddened them. I could tell by the look on their faces. "I must leave now for a brief time, but soon I will return and then I will take my place again with you by my side. Take care of this store, keep doing her justice. Stick to our formula. Do not get caught up in the delusion and fashion of the day." The owner then departed the scene.

Every evening, at the closing of the store, one could see the staff staring into the distance to see if he was returning from his trip. His promises were always sure. His word was secure. Their years of working together, his care as the owner, had always proved outstanding. They missed him, but he would return.

Over time, however, the customers began to become impatient. The absence of the owner dissatisfied them. As a result, sales also plummeted. According to the latest fashion, the brides preferred to dress a little more bluntly, lasciviously, multi- colored. The old-fashioned and dated long dresses no longer seemed to appeal to the crowd. People passed by the shop window without looking. The bell that announced the arrival of a customer was heard less and less.

Four years passed, and the staff was still waiting for the owner. They felt a growing urgency; the bridal store might go out of business! The owner might want everything to stay the same, but the customer is always right! White, clean, covered, pure with no fuss was perhaps completely out of date. Besides, would not the owner want them to take matters into their own hands to save what could be saved? They could not let the place go bankrupt without a fight, could they?

The staff got carried away by the fashion of the day. Times change, it was time for them to change. If they could make the clothing appealing again, the owner would also return. Perhaps he had heard of the demise of his store from hearsay and that was why he stayed away for so long, out of shame!

One evening, after closing time, they taped newspapers to the storefront windows to change the collection. The white covering dresses were taken off the mannequin and replaced with trendy and new alternatives. The skirts were shorter, the cleavage much deeper than the owner would have allowed. Posters showing ladies in bridal lingerie were put on the billboard that stood in front of the store during opening hours.

The evening was ending, the transformation of the store was complete, and the staff could not wait to turn over the Open sign the next morning. The people who passed the store daily would not be able to believe their eyes now that the simple-looking dresses had given way to a much more exciting line of clothing with sensual accessories. The owner would surely be proud of how they had acted to save the store from bankruptcy.

As they were getting ready, full of excitement, rushing to reopen the store the next day, they were unaware that the owner had returned from his trip that very night. The paper on the windows puzzled him. Why wasn't anyone allowed to see his beautiful white dresses? He could not wait, after all this time away, to hear his key turning in the squeaky keyhole to run his beloved store again. When he opened the door, smelled the *familiar scent of his store, and turned on the lights, doubt struck him. He was as restless as an animal lover in a room full of hunting trophies. Was this his bridal store? Had he really left it like this? What he saw was vulgar, flat, lascivious, a spectacle, dirty and stained.*

The sun was already rising, and it would not be long before people would be walking down the shopping street. He went through the store like a man possessed, taking everything that displeased him and tearing it to pieces, crying, and throwing it in the dumpster. He retrieved the sheer, white dresses from the backroom of the store, blew the dust off the beautiful designs, and carefully placed them over the mannequins in the window and on the shelves of the store.

Now it was time to pull the newspapers from the window display and clean the window. With sweat on his brow, he was about to pull off the first newspaper when he heard the door creak that rang the bell. He was no longer alone. There stood his staff, ready for another day of work. The look in their eyes consisted of a mix of joy, fear, and anxiety. They were happy to see the owner again after all these years, but there was something on the look on his face that made them shiver. The owner climbed out of the shop window, looked at them with a sad but determined look to ask them only one question: "What have you done with my store?"

That was the dream, Martinus. Not surprising that such a thing makes one restless between day and night, don't you think? When I handed him back his notebook, his explanation followed.

"Dear Sister. What do you think the owner did to his staff to whom he had entrusted his store? I will tell you. I think he had them come to him one by one, held them accountable for turning his store into something terrible, and then he fired them on the spot.

"This is what I think God wants to make clear to me with this dream and you just must see for yourself if there's some wisdom in

it. All those new methodologies, programs, books, or spiritual golden boys who come over from all corners of the world and seem to conquer their predecessors are nothing more or less than the staff who want to spruce up the store so that the residents of the city will set foot across the threshold again. They are turning the church into something it should never be. Attractive to seekers, but at the same time shabby to those who have already found and are content. It is food for the goats, but the sheep are starving. The church should be attractive to God, not to the surrounding culture, if I can put it bluntly.

"We are all called here not to liven up the store, but to prepare it for the return of the owner. I think He has clearly shown us how He would like to see His congregation when He returns. Spotless, clean and without blemish and other imperfections. I sometimes wonder, Sister, if He is right to put something so precious partly in our hands, but surely, He knows what He is doing, don't you think? It is up to Martinus and up-and-coming talent like me here to lead, equip, correct, encourage, and teach the congregation as He has told us to do when He left for a short indefinite time. No less is asked of us; certainly no more!

"You can say a lot of things about Martinus, sister. I understand that too, especially now, but he is someone who preserves the store. He does not get carried away with all the new tricks and gimmicks of this age. He's not a reed shaken by the wind. I think you should listen to him and let him do his business. Can I get you a coffee, sister? Nice little book by Mr. Hybels. Still of impeccable character after all these years, we cannot say that about our own shepherd, can we?!"

CHAPTER 9

THE HEARING

Now that Lydia had seized the car, there was nothing else to do but to arrange a driver for the long drive to the province of Utrecht for the hearing of my case. Case was, of course, heartily willing to put his VW at my disposal and himself as travel companion and private driver. On the condition that he would drive without "pops and bangs," I took him up on the offer.

"You'll never guess what I read in the paper today at Sr. Wierenga's house, Pastor. Do you know that they want to replace people like you and me by robots soon? It seems that within twenty years, they think they will get to the point where the Pastornator 2024 XL will see the light of day. Just wait, I have the little article here somewhere for you!"

With one hand on the steering wheel and his gaze on the back seat, he delved through the mess. The backseat was full of empty bags of M&M's, half-full bottles of Pepsi, a roll of toilet paper, and a clipping from the Dutch newspaper that day. Exactly how he managed, while searching, to keep driving dead straight and even shift from the right to the left lane to overtake someone remains a mystery to me to this day. I quickly snatched the article out of his hands so he could get back to more important things, like getting us safe and sound to the town of Doorn, and read the brochure of the Pastornator 2024 XL.

* * *

Congratulations on your purchase of the Pastornator 2024 XL. This robot pastor not only looks great but is also capable of producing authentic sounds. Unlike your human shepherd, it is safe to pet and cuddle him. The Pastornator 2024 XL always keeps his hands to himself.

Well, I thought, *at least this is one form of technology that is helpful.* So that hearings and transgressive behavior will be a thing of the past in twenty years!

When delivered, the Pastornator 2024 XL *defaults to standby mode, just like the flesh-and-blood variants. With a gentle pat on his back, he becomes active. There is a chance that he will babble incoherently for the first few minutes. Our advice is to let him rave for a while. After about five minutes, the storyline will start to become detectible and via the listen-back function, you can still decipher the opening sentences.*

You have chosen the male variant. This one is super easy to use. In particular, he responds extremely well to positive feedback. To promote longevity, it is wise to give him an elevated place so that he has plenty of opportunities to look down on others.

In addition to the Pastornator 2024 XL *the contents of the package include a brush with which his hair can be combed into any desired model. As one of the first users, you will receive three different clothing sets to dress your robot pastor according to the church denomination (see section Additional Modules) in which he will make his appearance, more on that later.*

***Warning!** Never put the* Pastornator 2024 XL *in full light. There is a good chance it will blow itself up with dire consequences. It thrives best in the shade.*

As promised, you will receive three additional modules that you can install through its backend. Try not to think too much about this. These modules allow you to choose which sermon style and theology suits you on any given Sunday. Below is a brief overview.

Module Pastornator 2024 XL Baptist

When inserting this module, you will notice that the Pastornator 2024 XL *becomes waterproof. In addition, it creates the ability to raise the hands to different degrees. Our three favorite modes are: "How big is my fish?" "Lion King," and "Rocky."*

This variant charges fastest in an environment where songs are sung with a lot of unnecessary repetition. In terms of clothing, the Baptist module matches best with set I consisting of a hipster beard, checkered shirt with loose buttons, tight jeans, and white trainers. As a bonus, it is possible to make him suddenly disappear while his clothes remain. Try this during a sermon series on the end times. Success guaranteed. To do this, press the LB buttons simultaneously.

Module Pastornator 2024 XL Reformed

After installing this module, little seems to change, his movements remain stiff and rigid. However, when you place it on the pulpit, you will hear that the voice becomes several octaves lower and takes on a lilting, threatening tone. Have no fear. You can turn this variant off remotely via the red button should he get too out of hand.

As a bonus, we have pre-loaded the 52 Sundays and 129 questions of the Heidelberg Catechism, including all the answers. This variant recharges fastest in a dusty library without fresh air and a view of the outside and plenty of comfort food within reach. In terms of clothing, it is best to go for set II consisting of a three-piece pinstripe suit, white shirt, and inky-black tie. Should you wish to take him on vacation for a lecture at a Reformed campsite, you can dress him in the specially added, pinstripe swimming trunks, worn over the knee, which we have added as a bonus.

Module Pastornator 2024 XL Charismatic

After adding this module, you will soon find that this version is effortlessly capable of imitating both other modules. Nevertheless, we have added two extras for your convenience. You will see that the right hand of this version is able to forcefully push over your congregants in no time. In addition, with a gentle tap on the back, it is possible to make gold dust swirl out of his eyes that will fall right into his Bible. The clothing set that goes well with this module is set III, consisting of a slightly too tight tailored suit, double Windsor tie, three gold teeth, private Playmobil airplane and a Lego cash register system. A pair of pants with extra deep pockets, for when the robot needs to preach at a conference, is included. As a bonus, you will receive a chair that can be placed in any mall to pray for leg-length difference next to a robot Barbie to accompany him on any distant travels.

We hope you enjoy your purchase, and we will continue to innovate this product in such a way that hiring a paid pastor becomes a blast from the past!

Often, I could laugh at Case's mischief and his ability to take himself and his future profession a little less seriously than the things of God himself, but that day I was not in the mood. I was tense, had not eaten anything all day, and had a knot in my stomach. The phone call, the indictment, the adventure with the hamster and missing Lydia and the kids had their effects. I was uncertain of what was to come. The miles of highway passed us by, and not much more was spoken along the way other than the essentials.

We drove into Doorn, just in time, and the gravel crunched under the tires as we braved the driveway of the Baptist administrative center. As pastors among ourselves, we sometimes jokingly called this "the ivory tower of Babel." They have been here for decades, giving answers to questions we do not ask, in ways we do not understand. They are like principals who have never been in front of the classroom themselves. Pastors who have never lasted more than six months anywhere, only to disappear forever behind the desk to tell those who do last how to do their jobs.

I wriggled out of the seat and unbuckled the double belt. I sucked the clear, fresh air into my lungs. I felt a shiver running through my spine and tingly sensations in my hands and back, my heart beating irregularly in my throat. My mental limit had been reached and, since I am not much of a talker, my body gave the first signals. Case put an arm around me, like the big, strong brother I never had. He promised to defend me and eat them for breakfast. I warned him that his silence might be more beneficial to my cause than his speaking, but he seemed unimpressed, adamant.

Together, we entered the stately building. A national monument that hung like a millstone around our annual denominational budget, but for now, no one was considering getting rid of it. A beautiful marble floor, a wooden spiral staircase. A series of photographs, beginning in black and white and slowly transitioning to color. Serious looking men, most of them wearing black glasses. All chairpersons of yesteryear. The faith heroes of our denomination. I'd read books by most of them, really learned something from some. Not so much because of what they said, but from how they lived their lives. Their biographies were inspiring; one will never be written about me.

Case nudged me, "Shall I put your picture here too, Pastor? I'll put a note next to it, 'Wanted: Dead or Alive for attempted sexual assault.'" I did not have the energy to reprimand him for his successful attempt at gallows humor.

The receptionist was waiting for us and took us to a waiting room where we took a seat until we were called back. Coffee, black, just the way we wanted it, was served. After a few minutes, we were taken by the executive secretary and asked to come with her to one of the many meeting rooms in the building. As we walked in together, I saw the three-member board seated. "They look like dead people on leave, Case, don't you think?"

"I think you're right, Pastor."

At the back of the room was a slightly raised stage, to exude authority, where they sat in their small wooden chairs. Three plastic bottles of water, a couple of notebooks, and a pencil case was all they had on the white tables they hid behind. As if they were afraid that they would soon be hounded by the Drent and his master.

Surprised, they look at Case, who had put on his army boots and a pair of shorts with holes in them for the occasion, to remove any doubt that he could be my lawyer. It took time to convince the board that he should be allowed to join in. Eventually, they agreed because they did not want to deprive him of the learning experience.

"Glad you are here, Martinus. Case, I hope you feel welcome too. The reason we are together is, of course, less pleasant. It pains us, Martinus, that of all the under shepherds, we see you sitting here across the table. The Crown Prince among preachers seems to have fallen from his high horse." As the president, positioned centrally, took the floor, I saw the brethren on his left and right smiling affably. The critical reports I had written regularly over the past few years about the degradation of our denomination and the liberal winds I saw blowing through the seminary seemed to be returning to my face like a boomerang. Physician, heal thyself! I hear them think.

"All right, to the point, gentlemen. The charge is attempted sexual assault. To be honest, we did not think you would be capable of such a thing, but this probably is the way you deal with the stress of the ministry nowadays. Sr. Saskia van Houten, well known to you, was here last week to explain her accusation. You allegedly kissed her on her forehead and pulled her tightly against you. By doing so, you insinuated that you desired more than just comforting her. A clear transgression of the preestablished boundaries, Martinus. Treating a young, vulnerable divorced woman like that is asking for trouble. You should know better after all these years of service," the chairperson concluded patronizingly.

The man to his left added that it seemed it was me who needed comfort and not her. He was the HR person of the board and might have read in my personnel file that I had been honest enough during my PDP interview to tell them my marriage had fluctuated between hills and valleys in recent years. All three gentlemen got on my nerves as the clock ticked on.

When I stood to give an account of the ruins that were in me, I was hard-handedly pushed back by Case, who boldly spoke up. "Gentlemen, I need to get something off my chest.

There seems to be no warmth here. Especially for a group of people who claim to love each other as Jesus loved us. I get the idea that Martinus is brought before the twenty-first-century equivalent of the Sanhedrin, consisting of three old crows who have absolutely no feeling for what he is going through here. It seems that, in your opinion, he is already guilty before his guilt is even proven. But you might be barking up the wrong tree here."

The men stretched their necks and looked at the Drent like ostriches with bulging eyes. "We are going to play a little game together before Martinus speaks, and I will not tolerate any pushbacks from your side, okay? We have earned a little entertainment after such a long drive, haven't we?" Case reached into his backpack and took out two items. He walked to the raised podium with his size forty-six army boots and placed the items pontifically in front of the chairman while continuing to stare at all three of them.

"We start easy today: What do we see lying here, gentlemen?"

"An obsolete Polaroid camera and a more expensive Canon video camera, Mr. Parker. At least, that is my first guess," spoke the man to the right of center, his hands crossed, leaning back, still with an affable smile.

"Spot on, brother. I can see that I am in the presence of giants. So, I do not need to ask you what the difference is between the two: the Polaroid gives a snapshot, the Canon records the facts measured over a longer time." On the other side of the table, there was a bored nod.

"Let me say this to you today, in defense of Martinus here. In short, this is the error of judgment you are making right now. You are judging Pastor here on a Polaroid and not on a video recording." The men looked at Case, uncertainty marking their features. By then, I already knew where Case was going because

I used this example during one of my performance reviews with him at Sr. Wierenga's table.

"The Bible, and I assume you hold that book in high esteem, cuts right through marrow and bone. It brings up what is down and brings out what wants to stay in. We read in it that we should examine ourselves whether we are in the faith or not and that we should bring forth fruit of repentance. At least, that is taught at the seminary, the same seminary that is under your responsibility, correct?" Without waiting for their answer, Case continued. The tension was almost palpable. An uncomfortable shuffling of chairs had begun behind the table.

"Now then. You will have to agree with me that the Bible, when it comes to self-evaluation, always speaks of a walk of life measured over a longer time and not a snapshot. God does not look at Polaroid photos, but evaluates our lives based on lifelong video recordings, all recorded and stored on the heavenly hard drives. I reckon that all of us, you included, have had moments in your life when you sowed in the field of the flesh instead of the field of the spirit. Situations when you were hopelessly out of line in word, deed, or meditations of the heart. A trivial lie, an unkind word, those kinds of things. Now, suppose a Polaroid picture were taken of you at your worst moment and the photographer was able to show that picture to God Himself: Would you stand the judgment, based on that picture?"

I was very curious what the men were thinking at that moment. Were they impressed by the young Drent's oratorical skills, or were they going back in their minds to their own hidden bosom sins? I could sense that they knew what I knew; there certainly was a grain of truth in all of this. It hit very close to home!

"I will satisfy your curiosity; based on that moment, you would be judged and found wanting. Unfit, written off, served off for eternity. You, along with Martinus and I here, will thank God on your bare knees that He does not take Polaroid pictures of His sheep, but judges them by their walk of life, and that with all of this he bestows grace upon grace, substantial portions of undeserved favor upon us. So, it would be good to relax for a moment, loosen up, take a deep breath from your diaphragm, and give some grace to the old gentleman in front of you. Then come out from behind that table on that stage, lower yourselves for a moment to our pitiful level, and then we will give thanks together for the generous grace and radical forgiveness that is within Christ."

All three remained seated, looking uncomfortably at everything around them, just to avoid eye contact with Case and me. That must have been how the men who had picked up their stones and brought their hands into the throwing position to stone that adulterous woman had stood.

"If we were to watch the video recording of Martinus's life for a moment, however, we would find many surprises, crazy and funny things too, I think. Yesterday he resuscitated a hamster for a small child. You would not have thought that he had that in him. It would reveal that the events of June 14, 2004, are not normative for his spiritual life or the performance of his position as an under-shepherd. Let me just say that I would encourage you to pass on horizontally what you have received vertically, namely grace and mercy.

"Without thereby erasing June 14 from his book of life, sin remains sin. A measure of punishment and discipline seems appropriate to me, but if he is truly deeply repentant about what happened with Saskia, I think that with a few very good conversations we can come a long way, don't you think, gentlemen?"

There was silence in the room. I wondered if I should have mentioned to Case beforehand that these three men, after his internship, will also have to decide whether he will receive a vocational placement with the Baptists.

The silence lasted uncomfortably long. Case directed a serious look toward the stage where the three were feverishly pondering their next move. This profound lesson from a hillbilly Drent was not in the playbook they had rolled out of their energy efficient toner-saving laser printer in triplicate this morning.

"Very well. Case, thank you for your contribution. We will take it into consideration." The chairman spoke after clearing his throat. "But of course we are gathered here to hear from Martinus what he has to say. He does not need an intern to wipe his own path clean. We would like to give you the opportunity to speak, refute the charges, and give us your perspective on what happened that morning." With a hand gesture, the chair invited me to stand up and speak. He had regained his strength and was ready for round two.

All sorts of things went through my mind at that moment. For nights I lay awake thinking about my response. I played the movie back in my mind. Could it indeed be interpreted as attempted sexual assault? Had I really gone in way over my head? Surely there was not that much going on, was there? Surely this was all a storm in a teacup.

It felt like the rest of my life and career depended on how I was going to spend the next few minutes. But for me, in particular, my integrity was at stake, not so much outwardly, but inwardly. Could I still look at myself in the mirror if I started twisting things around here? What would Saskia think if I made a different representation? Would she still want anything to do with me? Would Lydia ever take me seriously again, or myself, if I would be acting holier than the Pope here, declaring before the full board that even looking at other women is foreign to me?

I found myself in a deep state of agony. Various defensive tactics crossed my mind. Suppose I went my favorite beat-around-the-bush route and denied everything. My track record and quick tongue would trump Saskia's interpretation of June 14. Result: I would be reinstated and could move on as if little to nothing happened. Saskia would be dismissed as a promiscuous woman, seeking conflict, and would be removed from church and everything would be back to normal. Surely there is another church where she could start all over again, right?

But suppose I go along with Saskia's story and say that it did indeed happen as she says. Chances are Lydia will leave, trust is gone, and my career will end. A visitation arrangement with the kids was my worst nightmare. I did not want and could not do without them. Contact with Saskia would remain good though. Maybe something beautiful could blossom with her from the ruins of all of this?

I finally realized that reality was even more horrific than the story Saskia stated here, in this same room. Indeed, if I looked deep inside, June 12 was a mere taste of who I really was and what could have happened if no one had sounded the alarm.

See, fantasies and soul-stirrings of the unwise kind lie somewhere at the bottom of everyone's heart. Nestled in the seabed, hidden from the naked eye. Above them are hundreds of feet of ocean holding them in place. Gradually, unfortunately, mine seemed to detach from the bottom with increasing frequency and were making their way upward. Some floated awfully close under the surface and the contours became visible to someone who looked a little deeper to break through my façade, like Evert Wierenga used to do and now, I assumed, the young Drent.

I had become afraid of my own thinking. For the things that I, in my mind at least, was capable of. Who could give me the rock-solid guarantee that it would stop with thoughts and that I would not one day pull these things to the surface and act upon them? That they would evolve like a shark targeting an unsuspecting surfer? God forbid that this would ever happen, but I began to consider it more. Dr. Jekyll was turning into Dr. Hyde.

Suddenly, I realized that this hearing presented me with a fantastic opportunity. A kind of hidden blessing, a golden prospect, a way out. For myself and all the people I could hurt because of my potential wrongdoings. The local body of believers would be spared a lot if I just let myself be led to the slaughter. Lydia's suffering would end. My decision was settled; not even the Drent's plea could change that.

"Brothers. I thank you for the opportunity to defend myself against what I have been charged with. I do not agree with the accusation of attempted sexual assault. Having said that, I must honestly confess that, in my mind, I have committed bigger sins than that. I am afraid that I am of little value to our denomination. I am over the hill. Eventually, I will be here again, then perhaps for a more serious offense. I have fought but lost. Struggled, but gave in to my dark side. Just ask Lydia. This is not the first time I have stumbled hopelessly in this area of my life, and I believe it will not be the last. I am well past my glory days; it will be downhill from here on. I am unable to keep the straight and narrow path. This is where I would like to leave it for now. Thanks again for having us. Case and I will not take up more of your precious time." I sighed. I had just nailed my colors to the mast. That was it.

I could see the zeal of the three of them to write everything down. They looked like squirrels frantically gathering nuts for their winter hibernation. That's how fast their hands moved across the paper. They were on a witch hunt and managed to catch one. They were preparing the stake.

Case was paralyzed. He did not utter a word for the first half hour on the road. Not speaking until we reached the A28 highway, and he was able to put his car in fifth gear. "Pastor, with all due respect and reverence, but have you completely lost your mind? How do you get it into your blunt head to bring yourself in to those creeps, just like that? I gave you a fantastic chance to score. The opponents were already down Martinus, the goalkeeper nowhere to be seen. Why on earth do you deliberately waste the opportunity to put everything right in a nanosecond?"

Steam was essentially coming out of Case's ears. His cheerful disposition was nowhere to be found. He was furious, out of his mind, a holy displeasure took hold of him. "Why do you set the bar for yourself so high, Martinus? Do you really think that those men have never looked where they should not look and that their motives and ambitions are always pure? Anyone who sets the bar as high as you do must be losing out. Do you think you are the Messiah? That you should walk through life sinlessly, be perfect? Are you that high up? Remember this, my friend, the last time God called a Messiah He did not knock on your door, okay?"

The Drent looked me menacingly in the eye as if he intended to unbuckle my seat belt and open the passenger door in one move to make me kiss the tarmac. His blunt criticism triggered something in me that almost made me want to do the same to him. I was at a physical disadvantage, but the rising anger in me would make up for that. Now it was my turn. There was life in the old dog yet!

"Wake up and smell the coffee, son. Who do you think you are, spoiled brat! Lecturing me like that?" I shouted in his left ear. "A few years of taking exams in a classroom and talking quasi-intelligently to each other in a dorm about lofty theological themes does not give you the right to lecture me.

What do you know about the shoes I am standing in? Man, you are like someone who, in a foxhole on the training grounds, tells you what you should and should not do on the battlefield without having any experience of hand-to-hand combat. You are still green as grass, boy! It is easy for you to talk from the sidelines. With Deborah, everything is still fun and new. You have no children, are just on your way with God. Everything is going well for you. Who can say if you are still thriving after twenty years? Maybe you will drop out after only five! Show a little more respect!" I felt my breath quicken, my blood almost rising to boiling point as I let it all out with my student.

We remained silent for a while. Case managed to deescalate the situation with one of his brilliant questions. "You know what you need, Martinus? A milkshake to cool down and clear your mind. We would both benefit from a cease fire, don't you think? A fight here along the A28 would not end well for you. Lydia would have to recognize you by your shoes if she ever came back."

I placed my hand on his knee as a peace offering and let out a deep sigh.

Until that day, I had never tasted a milkshake or seen a McDonald's from the inside. At the McDrive, it was time to place the order. Case ordered a super-sized BigMac with two half-liter Cokes for himself. "And for Martinus, here, a large banana milkshake. Maybe you can throw in some Diazepam. He's quite a piece of work today."

We ate and drank in the parking lot and then decided to get ice cream inside. As we were talking about Case's sermon for the Sunday ahead, a curious older lady approached us. "Say, I hear you talking about a sermon. Are you a pastor, perhaps?"

"I am, ma'am. I don't know for how long, but, as of now, I am indeed a minister of the Word, as they so nicely call it."

"Fine for you, say, then I want to ask you something I

cannot get my head around. My husband would like to get a tattoo, but we also go to church. Aside from the fact that I find it ludicrous that he would have such a horror placed at an advanced age, I wonder if there is not a verse somewhere in the Bible that prohibits tattoos. Could you help me convince my husband, Pastor?"

Without thinking, I decided to dust off an old joke my father used to tell. "Rest assured, ma'am. I have a tattoo myself, nothing to worry about. Your husband could theoretically make it to heaven with some ink under his skin."

The woman was clearly surprised and asked me the question I was secretly hoping for. Young Case could not take his gaze off me. "That surprises me pastor, what kind of tattoo do you have and where did you get it done?"

"I had a very small mouse placed on my right buttock, ma'am. You are welcome to see it if you want."

Case fell from one surprise into another now that he realized that stiff Martinus had placed a tattoo of a mouse on his derriere.

"Well, if it's not too much trouble, Pastor, I'm curious now," she said in an excited voice.

I unbuckled my belt and lowered my pants slightly. "Do you see it, ma'am?"

"No, preacher, I don't see anything."

"Oh well, that's too bad for you. I think it just crawled into its hole."

She looked as white as chalk. Case laughed so hard he burst into tears as the old lady put on her coat, slung her purse over her shoulder, and quickly left the restaurant with a look of disgust on her face.

CHAPTER 10

STIRRING BEHIND THE FRONT DOOR

That same evening, Lydia called. I heard Peter and Elizabeth playing with Grandpa and Grandma in the background, enjoying the full attention they deserved and received too little from me. No doubt they sensed that things were not going well at home. I deeply regret not having done what I had promised. Being there for them and providing them with a loving home during their early teenage years.

Lydia sounded tense, agitated. I did not blame her. She came straight to the point and asked about the hearing. Whether I had been honest or whether my smooth defensive talk had fooled the board. Whether I also managed to debunk Saskia's story. "Will it end with a hiss, or will you go out with a bang, Martinus? Is this marriage of ours just a house of cards?" she asked suspiciously.

The good thing about arguing over the phone is that you do not have to dodge looks and the other person cannot see your nonverbal communication. I always found it easier to tell the truth over the phone than in someone's face, still do. You only hear the effects of your message; you do not see them.

"I could really care less what you said or did not say,

whether you managed to save your own and our skin. What I think is most important Martinus is: Are you still thinking about Saskia? And when you think about her, what do you think about?" That question came as a surprise, like a left hook in a hitherto trouble-free telephone boxing match.

I was reminded of what a highly respected Reformed Bible teacher once confided to me about confessing sin. "The sins committed with hands and feet you must confess to those around you whom you have hurt with them. The sins of your heart and mind you only need to confess before God." I must say that that advice has stayed with me my whole life and was very convenient to me. That way I could experience and perform all sorts of things in my parallel world of thought without ever having to tell anyone, as long as I managed to refrain from them in real life.

Yet, that day, I chose to break the mold. I had been honest with the board, with Case, and more importantly, with myself. My inner and outer person were finally aligning. I could practice what I preach after all. Today I would be honest with Lydia. Honesty lasts the longest, my parents used to say. They were right. Honesty can also destroy a marriage.

"Yes Lydia, I still think about Saskia regularly, and my thoughts are not always of the clean kind. I struggle with that, and it feels like I am sinking in quicksand. Sometimes lust gets the upper hand inside, and I no longer want what God wants and what is good for us, Lydia. I am sorry, that is how it really is. I get increasingly disgusted with myself, and I'm unable to cut off Goliath's head. I can tell others exactly what steps to take, but I am not even capable of tying my own shoes in this area. I am a danger to myself, to the congregation, to you and the children, and to Saskia. This must stop."

That week I had read an interview of a pastor from overseas

who had been caught after years of adultery. He was asked about the deliberations of his heart.

"How could you continue to climb the pulpit all these years when you were entangled in an adulterous relationship?" he was asked.

"I will tell you how I was able to justify that. On Mondays and Tuesdays, I was disgusted with myself and the fact that my private and public life showed such a discrepancy. I then made a deal with God. I asked Him if He would give me the strength to make one more sermon for that Sunday. In return, I would then confess the adultery to my wife the following Monday, seek couples' therapy, and resign.

"That deal with God gave me so much relief that I could do sermon preparation on Wednesday, Thursday, and Friday without my conscience getting stirred. Then on Sundays, I would preach, as if it was my last sermon. People came to repentance, renewed their faith, were baptized, and I came home full of dopamine and adrenaline. Then I often thought on Sunday evening, 'Look, God is still using me in His service.' I guess I'm not that bad after all. I am still a useful tool in His hands. If I confess, I will lose the chances God gives me! That was just enough to keep on going with my wife and mistress, until the moment I was caught red-handed, and all deals and self-justification were thrown out of the window."

I was determined not to make any more deals myself. The time of cutting corners had to end. I nearly exploded inside with guilt and revolt. The great Martinus Metgod, Crown Prince among preachers, finally floored by all the rottenness underneath his gravestone and feeble walls underneath his plaster.

Lydia was furious after that confession. She scolded me, rightly so. I didn't expect her to hold out the olive branch. I fervently hoped that Grandpa and Grandma had taken the children outside by now. I was getting what I deserved. She ended the conversation, another step toward the raging sea. I plopped down, bewildered, after this new sledgehammer blow.

As a Baptist pastor, I was not familiar with the ins and outs of the spiritual warfare until that evening. Surely that was something more for my esteemed Pentecostal brethren. But it seemed I was throwing out the baby with the bathwater. We had all just recovered from the Toronto Blessing and other "fires" brought from North America to "set Europe on fire for Jesus." That made us Bible believers a tad too cautious.

But looking back on this evening, I, too, had to acknowledge that there must have been a strategic meeting in the spiritual realms. The location must have been somewhere between hell and earth, where the demons planned to end Martinus Metgod once and for all. His marriage, his fatherhood, his ministry. They would not rest until I was razed to the ground.

As I was recovering from the conversation and staring out the kitchen window, the doorbell rang. It was already dark, and I could not think of a church member who was in such distress of the soul that they needed to see me. Nor had I heard a VW Golf with a double exhaust pipe coming down the cobblestones. Case and I had seen and heard enough of each other for today and had parted ways hours earlier.

I decided to look and open the door. There she was. She was casually dressed, wearing makeup, as if getting ready for a date. Her lips were red, her eyes fixed upon me. Two cappuccinos and an apple pie filled her hands. She asked whether she could come in for a moment. I hesitated, and she sensed that doubt. This was a David and Goliath situation.

"Don't you like seeing me, Martinus?" Saskia asked, tilting her head slightly.

"Yes, certainly I like to see you, but for that very reason, it might be good that you don't come in." There was too little persuasion in my words; she seemed content with nothing but coming in.

"Cappuccino and pie are a cure for just about any nasty thing, you know. I think you could use some company and friendship. I heard you had to go to Doorn today. I was there last week. I would like to talk to you about that, if you will give me a few minutes. Is that possible?"

I capitulated and invited her in. She set the cake and hot drinks on the stairs and stripped off her fitted coat, which she hung over Lydia's spare coat. As if unconsciously, she was already taking her place.

I led her to the kitchen, and we sat down at the kitchen table. Enough distance between us, although that did not stop me on June 12. Where there is a will, there is always a way. I left the curtains open as a form of transparency. To straighten out for myself what was crooked.

"Martinus, I really regret this whole ordeal and how I behaved in June. When you kissed me, I had a flashback to my ex-husband and panicked. That is why I left so quickly that day. The words 'attempted sexual assault' were forced upon me by the board and in hindsight, I would have liked it to be quite different. I am sorry, you must believe me."

She was not to blame; she had been victimized, again, and I felt sorry for her. We drank our cappuccinos together, ate apple pie, and chatted about anything and everything. It was comfortable, like friends talking to each other, relaxed too.

Suddenly, there was a loud pounding on the door. My heart stood still. Lydia coming to get clothes for her and the kids? Could she have brought Peter and Elizabeth with her? Or my father-in-law. Even worse, maybe he was coming to sort me out... not to mention my mother-in-law! It would be the death knell, my worst nightmare. The knocking swelled. It was someone in a hurry. I walked quickly to the front door.

However, the silhouette I saw standing through the glass was larger. Case Parker. Storming in like a bull in a China shop, he strode toward the kitchen, grabbing Saskia's pink coat off the coat rack in one grab on the way. He sat down at the head of the table, right between us. He worked two slices of apple pie down in no time and acted all unconcerned. "Nice to see you Saskia, been awhile, hasn't it? Unfortunately, I think that pastor has forgotten that tonight he and I are leading the prayer meeting at Sr. Wierenga's home. Since he is without a car these days, I have come to pick him up. These clergy need a little help; Lord knows what they will be up to if they are left to their own devices for too long! I grabbed your coat. You can go. There is the door," he spoke sternly, resolute.

With an icy look, she met his gaze and grabbed her coat to leave. Hell had no regard for a stubborn Drent.

When Saskia closed the front door behind her, and I walked back into the kitchen bewildered, I saw Case looking at me with his arms crossed and a smile on his face. "So, Pastor, you do not waste any time, do you? Fortunately, Sr. Wierenga was walking her dog and could not contain her curiosity when passing your house. When she peeked in through the open curtains, she saw you sitting with Saskia. She immediately called me in to save what could be saved. Seems I was just in time."

I muttered that I had been caught off guard by Saskia's visit, that I was perfectly able to restrain myself, and that her visit was not planned. At least not by us here on earth. "If you say so, Martinus. I will let you be. Sr. Wierenga and I have another date today behind poor Arend's conifer hedge. At the thrift store, we managed to pick up a remote compatible with his new TV."

I thanked Case for coming and closed the door. It was time

to get in early; it had been an exhilarating and long day. Another stage had been added to my long agony.

Before going to bed, I received a text message from Saskia. "Next week I will be spending some days at the island of Terschelling by myself. Maybe you would like to spend a day or two together? I had meant to ask you that earlier on, but unfortunately, we were disturbed. I love being with you, Martinus. Think about it. Love Saskia." I decided to let the text sink in and answer tomorrow with a clear mind.

That night I dreamed a dream that Case could have dreamed. I was sitting somewhere in a beautiful wooden log cabin in a forest far from civilization. The fireplace was burning nicely, and there were two comfortable rocking chairs arranged around the hearth. Close enough to feel its warmth, enough distance to not get burned. A voice invited me to sit down. I sat alone at first, watching and listening to the crackling fire.

The door opened, and in the chair next to me sat someone I could not identify at first. It was a man, about sixty years old, maybe, and dressed in white. He handed me a book that I did immediately recognize. It was the Bible. He asked me to open it at Proverbs 5, and I fixed my gaze on him when I found the chapter. With a nod, he encouraged me to start reading it aloud. His eyes did not waver from me as I read about the destructive power of the strange woman. The call to drink water from your own well.

Those words reminded me of Case's dream about the fountain and the dump truck. The verse, "If anyone takes fire into his bosom, will not his clothes be set on fire?" pointed out to me the inextricable link between inner sin and the inevitable day when they are put into practice. I was warned of the adulterous woman who flatters me with her words, her inviting glance, her footsteps dragging me into the abyss, her hands made like a hunter to kill and wound. I closed the book and looked aside, his eyes still fixed tightly on me. Lovingly, but serious. "The ways of a man are before the eyes of the LORD; He carefully watches all of his path." I hear the Spirit whispering in my heart.

Suddenly, I heard a loud cry coming from outside the log cabin. A cry that rose above everything else. Together, we went outside and followed the forest path up a steep incline. The screams grew louder as we continued up the path. On top of a hill, under the moonlight, I saw her standing. It was Lady Wisdom who managed to drown out the strange woman's voice. "With Me is counsel and wisdom. I am insight, with Me is strength! From the beginning I belong to the LORD. I am His favorite child. Observe My ways, listen to My admonition, and become wise. Do not reject it."

Abruptly, she was gone. The silence was deafening. I was alone again, in the log cabin. In front of the crackling fireplace was a large bucket of water. I threw it on the fire, grabbed my things, and slammed the door behind me.

Sobbing and sweating, I woke up the next morning. Grateful that God had spoken. It felt like a fresh wind had blown through my life and blown away old leaves for good. Evidently, there had also been a meeting in heaven, and God was again a few steps ahead of the adversary. By first making Sr. Wierenga curious, then sending the Drent, to now speaking through a dream. This battle He had won gloriously. This precision rocket had defused the enemy's first attack.

But I fully realized that I wasn't out of the woods yet.

CHAPTER 11

THE ISLAND

It will not surprise you, my readers, that people soon got wind of the nature of my transgressive behavior. It proved difficult to keep everything indoors. The congregation was in an uproar when they learned that their beloved Sr. Saskia had become the vulnerable victim of my lack of self-control and carnal desires. Some had always known that I could not be trusted, or at least they trumpeted that around in and outside the church. To this day, I do not know who spilled the beans. Many church members revealed that it had not been them because the Lord had placed a guard before their lips. Was it the board, my own elders, Case, or Saskia herself?

The result of this treason was that the next step of church discipline was instituted. I was suspended from all duties for an indefinite period. The situation seemed unsustainable. The net was closing in; pastoral termination was closer than ever. I was taking another few steps down, my toes able to touch the icy water.

Although the dream set me right back to my feet, helping me to gradually return to my first love, as the Bible so beautifully says, the woman of my youth was not yet willing to return to me. I called her and asked her if she wanted to try again, indicated that I missed the children, but it was not enough to persuade her. Too much had happened. Saskia was the straw that broke the camel's back. Lydia not only earned the right to speak after all these years, but also to hit me with the consequences.

And so I decided to remain silent. Toward her, toward Case, toward the board. I did not want to speak and see anyone for a while. I closed the curtains. I was tired. I was exhausted.

I opened my laptop to go watch a DVD of the humorous kind. Over the years, I had lost my laughter a bit. The chuckle that puts things in perspective. I needed it desperately.

After entering my password, the notification that I had received a new email caught my eye. From Saskia. A picture of her on the boat heading for an island. The sun was shining, and her hair was blowing in the wind. The sea looked good on her. Just a short message: "Will I see you later in Terschelling?" I felt completely alone, torn between all kinds of feelings. I wanted to choose the good, to lay off the weak in me. Get rid of my thorn in the flesh once and for all.

I packed my things, put on my windbreaker and hiking boots, made a call and waited for what was to come. I remained outside, waiting for my taxi, and left without my laptop and phone; I did not need them for what I wanted to do. If only I had brought them with me, it would have saved me years of misery.

I went to Harlingen to take the boat to the island. I wanted to get a breath of fresh air, feeling the wind in my hair. No hassle for a while, pleasant company. I was looking forward to cappuccino, apple pie, and a good heart-to-heart exchange. This would be a new turning point in time. A new page in the life of Martinus Metgod, I imagined.

I bought two tickets. The boat that came to pick us up

docked. I could smell the salty sea, could see the waves pounding on the dock. I took the stairs down onto the boat, making my way up to the panoramic deck from there. We came off the wharf and sailed up the Wadden Sea toward the island, leaving behind the problems that belonged to the mainland.

Case had picked me up after I invited him to join me, and the drive up was hilarious. Men among themselves telling the smoothest stories to each other. Of course, only clean jokes were allowed, which is to be expected from a spiritual nestor and his apprentice.

Among other things, he told me about his first date with Deborah. "Pastor, our first date was at her older brother's house. He and his wife went out for dinner somewhere nearby, and Deborah and I got to watch their children. An evening on the couch, cuddling and watching TV, could not get any better, right? Well, I had consumed a hearty bean dish and soon had to do a number two, if you know what I mean." I replied that I had some idea what he meant by that. "Well, as it turned out, the toilet was clogged. There was no way I could flush the goo. After one-and-a-half hours of trying, Deborah and I decided it was time to go for plan b. With a plastic glove, I scooped everything out straight into the kitty litter box that Deborah had dragged into the hallway. After the toilet was empty and we had erased all traces, we dragged the thing back to the utility room as if nothing had happened. All is well that ends well, Martinus, don't you think?

"But when Deborah's brother returned home with his wife, he noticed that something smelled slightly different than usual. The stench was obviously coming from the litter box. 'Did you have something to do with this, Case?'

"I, of course, denied plainly and told a story about the processed food that cats sometimes ingest so that everything comes out at once through the back exit. It looked like I had sent my future brother-in-law up the garden path, but he proved to be unapologetic.

"'Sounds plausible, Case, but that leaves us with one intriguing problem. Something fascinating.'

"I looked at him sheepishly, long since glad I had covered my sin with cat litter and invited him to continue. 'Well, Case, our cat died six weeks ago, and it does not seem plausible to me that he has been posthumously defecating. I reckon that what I see and smell here has something to do with our clogged toilet.'

"Pastor, I had to confess that I was guilty. Every year, during the gifts exchange at St. Nicholas, they include a poem for me to read aloud in front of everyone present, and it always includes this story. This incident will haunt me all my life, far beyond Drenthe. Oh well, it is what it is, right?"

While tears of laughter streamed down my cheeks between Leeuwarden and Franeker on the A31, Lydia had burst into tears. She had driven to Zwagerheide to pick up some clothes for herself, Peter, and Elizabeth.

As she poured herself a cup of tea in the kitchen, her gaze fell on the open laptop. We had, digitally, no secrets and through a simple password she entered the wonderful world of my inbox. Saskia, with her long, blonde hair blowing in the wind, was the first thing she saw. Then she read the short message. She knew enough. When she read the text message on my phone from days before about a possible rendezvous on Terschelling, my plea was settled. Through internet banking, she saw today's debit from Wagenborg passenger services, and my goose was cooked. The absence of my windbreaker, hiking boots, and backpack was the conclusive and shocking proof she needed. From that moment on, she, too, turned a new page, one without Martinus Metgod that is.

It would be years before she dared to confide in a man again. She was a sweet woman, a wonderful mother. She would fall in love again one day, I was sure. She had too much love to keep to herself. She would find herself another man who would truly do her justice. She deserved a new lease of life, and I am glad she got to taste the clear wine of love again in the winter of her life.

Unaware of Lydia's sorrow fifty kilometers away, Case and I headed for the island of Vlieland. We let the boat to Terschelling pass us by. Saskia would just have to enjoy herself; surely, she would find someone there who would give her the attention she needed. Maybe she would be disappointed that I did not show up, but maybe not. I would no longer be part of her little cat-and-mouse game.

At the beach, I decided to teach Case some valuable lessons. "Friend, your internship here has come to an end. I want to impress upon you the following: Please do as I have said, not as I did. The pastoral ministry is an outstanding work, but also a dangerous calling. I lasted about twenty years; the new generation sometimes throws in the towel within three. Think of it as a marathon, Case, and not a quick sprint to success." I addressed him as sand blew in my face.

"Pastor, may I ask why you talk as if you are on your professional deathbed? All is not lost. Stop that doom-and-gloom thinking of yours, and do not be so hard on yourself. We will get back on that little boat tonight, and you will stretch your shaky knees and straighten that rounded little back of yours, and we will give it another go, okay?"

I thanked him for his encouragement but assured him that my mind was made up. There was no time to get back to the drawing board.

"Case, if I don't stop being a pastor, my marriage will go to ruins, and I won't see the children again."

"Nonsense, Martinus, surely God will not require contrasting things of you? Surely, He is not asking you to place your family on the altar of ministry or vice versa. If God has really called you, they can both coexist." He assured me as he once again tested my upper arm with his right fist.

"I hope you and Deborah will succeed, Case, but I failed. In quick succession, I have just spent the past few days looking back at my entire life like a movie, and I am not happy with what I saw. My marriage is a disaster, and I barely spend any time with the kids. The last time I really did something with Peter was much too long ago. We carved a small wooden box with a Bible text on the importance of family devotions burned into it. Well, how hypocritical can you get?

"And do you know what Elizabeth said to her teacher the other day? 'Daddy doesn't have much time for me, he sits at his computer for a very long time every day writing a sermon for Sunday.'" Tears streamed down my cheeks as I confessed to Case page after page from my horrible biography.

The young Drent acted his role as confessor appropriately. Martinus Metgod as a cautionary example of how not to live the spiritual life. The pastor who found it difficult to distinguish between what he was and what he pretended to be. Who for years could not reconcile his will and that of his Lord in the most crucial aspects of his life.

"Case, just a quick admission on my part. You may have sensed it, but I must confess to you that I had little faith in you when I received your handwritten scribblings and we spent time together for the first time. But you surprised me, kid. You are special, just by being yourself. Will you promise me that you will run the race set before you? Will you assure me that when there comes a time when you think you have arrived, that you will be extra careful not to fall? Promise me that you will do everything you can to prioritize Deborah over your ministry. Guarantee me that you will not make the church and your work an idol. Workaholics are put on a pedestal in our line of work, but it destroys more than you care about. Take care of your own fountain, boy. Listen to the voice of Lady Wisdom. Maybe work on that strange Drenth accent of yours for a while, but other than that, please stay as you are."

Unexpectedly, he took hold of me, but I managed to free myself. The judo lessons in my youth came in handy. I took off running, but with his size forty-six feet, he had me where he wanted me in no time, on the ground. He lifted me up and threw me into the sea, laughing hard. "So, here you are, the first Baptist preacher to get baptized after his ordination. Wonder what they will say about that in Doorn, Martinus!"

I have many fond memories of that day on the beach. We decided to let me dry off somewhere at a beach restaurant while enjoying a hot chocolate with whipped cream. Once dry and back on the mainland, we had another milkshake in Leeuwarden to conclude a wonderful day and my remarkable year with Case Parker.

We ended the internship with one last cup of coffee at Sr. Wierenga's place where the Drent packed his things to go back home, where his heart was. With Deborah, his family of origin, the Drenthe countryside. With a pop and a bang from his exhaust, just as he had come, he left Zwagerheide. It was the first intern that made both Eugenie Wierenga and me shed a tear when he left.

After seeing him off, I walked back to my parsonage. The door was open; I thought, to my excitement, that I could smell Lydia's perfume, but she herself was nowhere to be seen. In the kitchen, to my distress, I saw the open laptop and my phone lying on the table. Our wedding photo lay in smithereens on the kitchen floor. On the table was a small note.

"I hope you had an enjoyable time at Terschelling with 'Sas,' Martinus. I am sure she gave you what you thought you needed. I certainly know my place now. Good luck and leave the three of us alone. You have already done enough damage. We can do fine without you; in fact, we have done so all these years. Lydia."

All my efforts notwithstanding, contact proved impossible. Lydia had left with an unknown destination. Nowhere to be found. Not even her parents knew where she was during that first month. Through an intermediary, I received the message that she had filed for a legal separation.

Case turned out to be my last intern. The suspension was converted into pastoral termination. Because of the nature of my offense, a transition pay was out of the question. No church wanted me anymore, but I had no problem with that. The congregation had its fill of pastors for now and decided not to hire a new under shepherd for the time being. An older, wise pastor a few villages down the road led them through a transition period and picked up the pieces. I agreed with the church treasurer that I could continue to rent the parsonage until either party had seen enough of each other. Neither I nor the church ever heard from Saskia again. She moved to another part of the country early after the board's ruling.

Now, almost twenty years later, I still live here. Dorpsstraat 18, Zwagerheide. Not much has changed, really. It's like stepping into a museum. Should a new shepherd ever be recruited, they will have to refurbish the place themselves; I will not bother. Winter is over. Spring is just around the corner; gray will turn to blue. Then He will truly make all things new.

That said, dear reader, dear Peter, and dear Elizabeth, not everything has stayed the same in those twenty years. In the cover of this final volume of my memoir, you will find two letters. At least, I hope so. There was quite a plague of mice raging here a few years back, and I cannot set any more traps posthumously, of course, you understand. Look inside the cover, take, and read. The first letter is for you and the other one is for Case and Deborah. I assume he is still with his first love and among the living.

I love you and always have, even in your absence. I hope we can spend eternity together. On the new heaven and earth there will surely be plenty of time to put the past to rest and enjoy a wonderful future together. Love, Dad.

Chapter 12

A Letter from Your Father, Martinus: A Beloved Child of God

Dear Peter and Elizabeth,

I am sorry that you had to grow up without your father. The first decade I may have been physically present, but in all honesty, you always had to do without me. I thought other things were more important. I was so terribly wrong. I cannot turn back time, and I do not blame you for never answering my cards and letters. You must be curious to know how I fared after this long agony and this remarkable year. What became of Martinus Metgod, that crazy father of yours?

I can say that in terms of my career, it went downhill. Though that's all water under the bridge now. Personally, I made a big step forward. I went down because of the church, but also came up again because of the church. As a church member at a neighboring congregation, I was able to keep a low profile. Less talking, more listening. I came to know God as a Father, rather than a strict employer, and that made all the difference. My first love for Him was restored. I hope this may happen to you too. I have continued to pray for you. That you will find the everlasting arms of the Good Father.

I have been forgiven, including for what I did to you. But

that does not take away the fact that I have had to bear the consequences of my actions for the rest of my days. The greatest loss I have suffered is the loss of your mother and the two of you. I will not tire you with what this has done to me, or you might even feel guilty. There is no reason to. You are not to blame. I am guilty, but blessed is He who came to bear that guilt.

I am also writing to solve another mystery for you. Sit back and hold on to your seats because this will surely come as a surprise!

I understand, from a reliable source, that you had the strong suspicion that there was a new man in Mom's life in the winter of her existence. My Lydia, your mother, has indeed fallen in love again. Up to her ears, I might add. That you never got to know him may be a loss to you, but Mom had an exceptionally good reason for that.

Seven years ago, on our wedding day she suddenly showed up on my doorstep. Time looked well on her, much better than on me. I was surprised, shocked. God had answered my prayers. I got the chance to talk about what had happened that day. About Vlieland, my day with Case, that I had resisted the temptation to sail to Terschelling to see Saskia. Mom cried.

We talked late into the night, cuddled up before the fireplace. We mourned the missed years, and the broken home, but also looked ahead to the days that remained. She wanted to stay the night, but on one condition: "Martinus, the children must not know about this. I want you, in winter, all to myself." She told me about her frail health, and the difficult road ahead of her, and we found comfort with each other and with the Omniscient One who numbered our days.

That entire year, dear children, was one big adventure. The man Mom occasionally spoke to you about was none other than your father. Not a new man, but a renewed man. We went to hotels together, walked in the park, spent time in the parsonage where she sneaked inside in the dark. We enjoyed the excitement and the sneakiness. Felt like two teenagers. We ended as we had begun. Head over heels in love, it was heavenly. I would not have missed that year for anything, neither would Mom.

On her deathbed in hospice, we thanked God together that he had restored our marriage, that he brought together what had been separated for all those years. That the best was yet to come for the both of us.

When she went to sleep, I left. I saw you driving into the parking lot as I made my way home just before you arrived. You were there when Mom went the way of all the earth. Together with you, I look forward to the day when He will say, "Behold, I make *all* things new."

I hope this final part of my memoir will help you. Do with it what you will. Maybe others can learn something from it. But this letter is for you alone.

My intentions were good; the execution often left much to be desired. Grace bought me free; grace also led me home. I so estimate that Mom and I now have an enjoyable time together and see Him who turned everything for the better. We are waiting for you. We can't wait to welcome you where we are, and that includes Him who kept all your tears in His jar, ready to wash them away for good.

Love, your father, Martinus Metgod.

EPILOGUE

After a restless night in which I and my wife, Ciska, had let our tears flow freely, I decided the following day to delight Elizabeth with this final volume of Father's memoirs, but especially with the letter Father had written with the breaking news that our parents had found each other again.

She read the memoir and letter in one go that morning, and the laughter won out over the tears. "Peter, what a handful, that mother of ours! Starting an affair with Father behind our backs without letting us know. Well, she certainly earned quality time with Dad. I would kill to leave my life with a dashing crush." Elizabeth is a delightful, uncomplicated thinker; I enjoyed how she could put all this in such a positive perspective.

For me, the balance still tipped a bit toward all those missed years, how different things could have been. That man did not have to die in solitude in that old parsonage.

"You and I are going to the ordination of that new pastor couple. I am intrigued about that Case and Deborah Parker, who will soon take over the congregation in Zwagerheide." Elizabeth spoke with determination.

I had not seen a church inside in ages; everything around church and faith breathed trauma to me. Nevertheless, I agreed.

We were given a friendly welcome by the church caretaker who had allowed us to vacate Father's home. A nervous couple with a couple of rebellious teenagers caught our attention. He was six feet tall; I heard a slight rural accent as he spoke to some other people who were also invited to this joyous event. He looked our way and recognized us as the rascals who had run about the parsonage. He was no longer as rough as father sketched him. By his own admission, he still drove a VW, but now a family car. A VW Touran. The conversation was pleasant.

Elizabeth gave him the other letter that was hidden in the cover of the memoir. When we wanted to take our place in the sanctuary, he asked us to stay, to read the letter with him.

Dear Case,

Hope you are doing well, boy. I was a little shocked by your last letter. Not so much from your ever lousy handwriting, but more because of your need to retreat in Ireland for a while. Do not forget to visit the Guinness factory in Dublin. You know how to properly pour a pint by now!

Now, I am no prophet and have no idea if you are reading this letter straight or years after this retreat, which depends a bit on how long my ticker will hold up. But I hope it brought you what you needed. For your ministry, but especially for your marriage. I hope you and Deborah are doing well. That you do what you promised me back then on Vlieland beach. It was great receiving your family photo. You married above your station, boy, and you know I know my business 😉. That photo got a nice spot on the mantelpiece here, next to Peter's, Elizabeth's, and my own wedding photo.

I wanted to personally let you know that Lydia and I have made up. It took twelve years, but we managed to end strong.

It is fair to say that even in our second term, we sometimes got stuck in the past. We always made up, however, invariably in the same place. Somewhere in a McDonald's where we drank a milkshake together. Those young people must have thought, what is an old couple doing at a fast-food chain like that? Oh well, we could not care less about that.

I prayed a lot for you, Case. Because of the pastoral termination, I had quite a lot of time to do that, and I assume my prayers helped you in ways you do not comprehend yourself. I prayed that you would keep running and not get tired. That you would finish the race. That you would always keep wearing your shorts and stubbornly refuse to fit into a straitjacket.

I enjoyed our remarkable year together. And your preaching at Sr. Wierenga's funeral. I sat as an accomplished spy in the back of the auditorium. She would have enjoyed that quote from Bill Hybels, boy! She and her Evert are now where Lydia and I are. I just assume that their joint struggle in getting me to adopt the latest church growth strategies is now over here in the heavenlies.

Stay safe, buddy. Zwagerheide has remained without a pastor all these years. I have followed the church from the sidelines. I have pointed out to the elders several times that they could well use a remarkable Drent there to liven things up. Who knows, maybe you'll follow in my footsteps here one day. Not in all of them, I hope, just in the right ones. Be kind to yourself, Case. We were like David and Jonathan, and I enjoyed every minute of it. You truly were a blessing in disguise. We will meet again, I am sure.

Heartfelt brotherly greetings,

Martinus Metgod, ex-Crown Prince of Baptist preachers, resuscitator of rodents, beloved of God, beloved of Lydia, father of Peter and Elizabeth.

Author's word

Dear Reader. As with my other books, you will ask yourself whether we are dealing with fact or fiction here. Let me be clear: I, a Baptist pastor myself, have not fallen into the intolerable and gross sin mentioned here. I have been happily married to Wieteke for twenty years and see my four children daily. I mention this disclaimer intentionally to avoid a family feud 😊.

So why a book on this theme? What we see with Martinus, I see happening in all sorts of places all over the world. Spiritual leaders falling, their names tarnished forever. Their books disappear from the shelves at Christian bookstores, their podcasts are taken offline, and what follows is a life in the lee. They are cancelled.

Let there be no mistake: A leader must be of impeccable character. Like Martinus, they must bear the consequences of their failures. Some have fallen so deeply that recovery, in ministry at least, is not possible.

Yet I wonder if, in our current cancel culture, we are not being too harsh by crucifying someone for their entire life after just one mistake. The list of people who are persona non grata seems to grow longer and longer.

Didn't we ourselves contribute to their fall? By naively putting them on a pedestal, by ascribing to them superpowers they do not have? Have we not expected, asked, and demanded too much of them?

Have we believed that a generation of leaders has emerged who were born before the fall? Who would outgrow the sins of David, Peter, Moses, Elijah, and Abraham? Who would be exempt from the seduction of the unholy trinity of money, sex, and power? Gold, girls, and glory?

I have resolved to be a little less harsh myself, without sweeping everything under the carpet. Under the cloak of love, things can get very smelly. The speck of dust in someone else's eye may cause me not to recognize the meter-long plank in my own eye.

Know this: If there is a plank in your eye, it is impossible to come close and become part of the repair work that the Heavenly Carpenter wants to do in every one of us, including fallen leaders.

I wish you the end of the journey of Martinus and the good cheer of Case. All the best to you. You will hear more from Case; I can tell you that! Find out more about his much-needed retreat in my first book: *The Retreat: A Lighthearted and Humorous Story about a Soul-Searching Pastor* and read more about his time in Zwagerheide, after his ordination in Book II: *The Heaven and Earth Conference: The Wondrous Diary of an Ordinary Pastor.*

Blessings,
Kees Postma.

Praise for Kees Postma

Kees Postma is a Dutch Baptist pastor and church planter living in the rural north of Holland. He likes playing his $50 guitar, watching good comedies, playing darts and going for long walks.

His favorite holiday destination is Ireland where he lived for over four years.

Please review this book
If this book has helped you in any way, please leave an online review at the retailer you bought it, on Goodreads or another platform. As a beginning author word of mouth really helps, especially in the niche that I'm writing for. Thanks again!

And why not grab Part 1 and Part 2 in the Case Parker Series? You can find them on Amazon and other retailers.

Printed in Dunstable, United Kingdom

70272299R00068